Tales
from a
Stone Cottage

Tales
from a
Stone Cottage

by *Aly Wilks*

Illustrated by Celia Witchard

To Carew, Mikey and Eddie, who
share the stone cottage. With my love.

And I'd like to thank Lisa Sykes
for her support and advice.

I also salute the villagers of Nettleton, West Kington and Burton,
happy in the knowledge that any resemblance between them and
the characters in these pages is entirely coincidental.

Text copyright © 2012 Aly Wilks
Illustrations © 2012 Celia Witchard

First published in the UK in 2012
by Quiller, an imprint of Quiller Publishing Ltd

Designed by Kath Grimshaw

British Library Cataloguing-in-Publication Data
A catalogue record for this book
is available from the British Library

ISBN 978 1 84689 148 9

The right of Aly Wilks to be identified as the author of this work has been asserted in
accordance with the Copyright, Design and Patent Act 1988

Printed in China

Quiller

An imprint of Quiller Publishing Ltd
Wykey House, Wykey, Shrewsbury, SY4 1JA
Tel: 01939 261616 Fax: 01939 261606
Email: info@quillerbooks.com
Website: www.countrybooksdirect.com

Preface

O n an auspicious day in 2007 I opened my *Country Living* magazine to read the following invitation: "Become our new columnist... We want to hear about your life in the country, the ups and downs, the changing seasons, the foibles of neighbours (if you dare) and your part in all this... The winner's work will appear in both *Country Living* and the website in September." It all sounded like my cup of tea and a few busy months later I did indeed become *Country Living*'s new columnist. Here is my very first column, published in September 2007: it sets the scene, meets the neighbours, introduces the stone cottage and demonstrates how it scored (and continues regularly to score) a perfect ten on the Cow Scale.

'Til the Cows Come Home

M y measure of personal happiness is the Cow Scale. The Cow Scale charts the likelihood, from nought to ten, of finding a cow in the garden. I invented it when I lived in army quarters; at the bottom (in every sense) was a German high-rise flat that scored zero: you're not going to get a cow in the garden – live with it. Best was a wind-blown semidetached on the Salisbury Plain that scored a seven: if a cow got out of the pens on the horizon and if it fancied the patch of scrubland that was my garden, it could happen. It didn't, but it could.

When we arrived here, I stood in the lane in a state of blissed-out shock, watching removal men attempting to lever the contents of an enormous van into a small, stone cottage.

Our stone cottage. I held a tea tray, because after 19 moves I have got the moving process down to a fine art. You supply tea, biscuits and loo paper in inexhaustible quantities, and you have happy removal men who do a lovely job and then plumb in the washing machine for you. I felt heavy breathing down the back of my neck, turned and looked straight into the faces of a dairy herd, which had assembled behind me en masse. They were like jostling groupies waiting for a boy band to arrive, but instead of crowd barriers there was merely a knee-high dry-stone wall. The chances of getting a good score on the Cow Scale were suddenly very high.

Rural life is about neighbours: love them or loathe them, you can't ignore them. Needing human company, I gravitated to the post office and shop, run by Anna, an angel in human form sent among us to do good. She introduced me to everybody in the shop. I was inspected and, after a thoughtful pause, somebody asked if I'd lost a ferret. I hadn't. In fact, I didn't have a ferret to lose. But I was so pleased to be accepted as the sort of person who might have lost a ferret. The man who asked was Maurice, who owned the dairy herd next to us, and had a touching faith in his mini dry-stone walls as cow barriers.

Fast-forward to the present. We are beginning to fit into the fabric of the place; we stick out less. I was back in the post office and Anna introduced me to Stephen, who is even newer – just arrived in the village. By rural osmosis I already knew his name, his wife's name, his dog's name, and the fact that his wife had been unimpressed with the cleanliness of their new bathroom when they arrived. "Do you usually have cows in the road outside your house?" Stephen asked me. "There were several there when I drove past just now!" Anna and I looked at each other. "I'll just nip home and check!" I said. "I'll ring Maurice," she promised.

I arrived home to catch a rear view of the dairy herd disappearing through our open gates and advancing into the garden. I scurried around the side and tried to encourage them back. A large matron rediscovering her inner calf, and pirouetting in the herb garden was just what I didn't need, so I was pathetically grateful when Maurice arrived, complete with an air of authority and a quad bike. Immediately, his cows stopped behaving like a hen party on a frisky night in Majorca and remembered their responsibilities as providers of quality milk to the neighbourhood, forming an orderly queue and retreating out of the garden at a dignified trundle.

Some of their parting gifts I scraped up, mixed into a glutinous soup with natural yogurt, and sprayed on the dry stone walls I'd just patched. Apparently, clumps of lichen will start forming in seconds (well, sooner than they would otherwise) and other wall plants will be gagging to grow on it. I can't do much about the patted gravel, except to hope for a heavy shower of rain. Very heavy. And I sprayed off the terrace so that we could sit out with a glass of wine and celebrate the fact that for the first time we were in a house that scored a perfect ten on the Cow Scale.

January

The January Sales

I was dividing the stable into deluxe maternity suites for my pampered ewes, with straw bales, when I became aware of an audience. Frank – local leprechaun look-alike and all-round countryman – was watching my struggles with detached interest and gave his verdict: "What you needs is hurdles!" Frank knows his sheep, and if he said I needed hurdles, then hurdles were what I needed.

Which was why I found myself a few days later in the yard of the cattle market, gazing at a pile of galvanised sheep hurdles. Over the other side, big men were grouped around a chunk of metal from which spikes stuck out. "Nice little acrobat," said the distant voice of an auctioneer, "what am I bid?" There was an enthusiastic quivering of catalogues, and I could see it would be some time and many implements later before the hurdles came under the hammer, so I decided to explore.

I ducked under a barrier and found myself in a barn, set out in long aisles of stacked cages. A 'supermarket' of sorts, but instead of sliced white and wine of the month, there was every variety of hen, duck and rabbit imaginable. I peered into a cage. Some glossy black hens with white ear patches stared back at me, without enthusiasm. Opposite them were ducks with a sign reading 'rear breed' [sic] tacked to their cage. They looked like all the other ducks, only more self-conscious. Next came hens with mad hairstyles that covered their eyes and a group of tiny bantams in pastel shades.

Close to a pen of aristocratic hens that could have posed for old-fashioned cigarette cards, was a cage containing what appeared to be a grey fluffy cushion. As I watched, it yawned widely and settled back to sleep. The end with the yawn had a large red comb, suggesting a cockerel. His cage door was suddenly opened and a golden hen five times his size was thrust in. The cockerel raised a bleary eyelid and took in her profusion of petticoats and frilly knickers. He did a double take and snapped awake. Obviously a bird of action, he gave a crow – HOT TOTTIE! - and hurled himself at her like a mountaineer tackling the foothills of the Matterhorn. A couple of men nearby were also examining the little cockerel and his lady. "I'll 'ave them for the ferrets," said one to the other.

At this moment, an auctioneer approached, trailing a crowd of potential hen-purchasers. "Nice little Lavender Pekin cockerel and a Buff Orpington hen – what am I bid?" "Fiver!" said Ferret Man. "Six!" squeaked a voice I dimly recognised as mine. "Seven!" said Ferret Man. "Ten!" I said, raising the stakes.

"Nah," said Ferret Man. "Going-once-going-twice-sold. Pay the lady in the booth," said the auctioneer, and they were mine. My adrenalin levels were now sky-high – I'd contracted auction fever. I scurried after the auctioneer and started bidding in earnest. I bought the 'rear breed' ducks and I bought the tiny, pastel bantams. I bought a pen of fantail doves with pink feet. I bought a pair of huge and belligerent geese and I bought a baby lop-eared rabbit.

Then the red mists cleared and I found myself standing by a pile of cardboard boxes filled with impulse buys. I peeked into the box containing my little Romeo with his massive Juliet. He was still keen as mustard, but she seemed only vaguely aware of the scuffling around her ankles. I went to have a celebratory coffee with the change left from my hurdle money. Then I remembered something and looked over to where the agricultural equipment had been. The remnants were being loaded into pick-ups and trailers. Whoops! I'd missed the hurdles.

Still, I drove my boxes home in triumph and distributed the contents around the cottage and garden. Romeo, Juliet and the bantams joined the happy crew in my hen ark. The geese moved into the orchard and began their reign of terror. The little rabbit joined our laid-back dogs as a house pet. Then I was brought up short by my lack of dovecotes and duck ponds.

Frank appeared, in supervisory capacity. I told him about my failure with the hurdles. "That'll be right," said Frank. "My mate Len's been making wooden hurdles for nigh on 60 years. He'll do some for you." Wooden hurdles… Now my maternity units would be deluxe and tasteful. I gave Frank the ducks and doves in sheer gratitude.

Snow Business

The first intimation I had that snow had come to the village was when I heard a muffled thump outside my bedroom window followed by a stream of colourful language. I looked out to a blinding white landscape and Frank, my neighbour, lying tangled up with his bike in a snowdrift. I rushed out to help, and Frank told me how, waking to find the snow falling heavily, he had set off to check his sheep. But his bike, usually so well behaved, refused to proceed in a straight line. "He ran me all over the road," said Frank, wide-eyed, "then he chucked me in your ditch."

As I commiserated with him, Mrs Addington's immaculate car came into view, sailed majestically past and approached the snowy hill out of the village. Halfway up, she deliberately stopped her car and got out. She locked the door and walked back down the hill, leaving the narrow lane effectively blocked. "Stupidly dangerous!" she snapped as she headed for home. Frank, too, set off very carefully in the direction of his sheep, wheeling his bike along the icy road.

I went to check on my own animals. My little flock of Shetland sheep were ignoring their cosy shelter with bulging hay rack, and were methodically using their feet to scrape away the snow from each grassy mouthful, just as their Scottish ancestors would have done. Jigsaw, my black-and-white cob, didn't want to go indoors either. She was having far too much fun rolling in the snow and charging at the few brave ramblers who used the footpath through her field.

My hens disapproved of their new white world and refused to come out of their ark, but the geese took advantage of the holiday atmosphere to bring their own particular brand of wilful assault to the wider community. Advancing in close formation through an unexpectedly open gate, they came across Maurice, our local farmer, bent double as he tried to pull-start his quad bike. Four beaks fixed simultaneously on the seat of his trousers as they exultantly scored the best combined hit of their careers.

I took refuge in the village shop where several other residents had already gathered, following some primal instinct to stock up with food in hard weather. We all agreed that the snow was lovely to look at, but you wouldn't want too much of it. Then Julia's snappy little sports car drove past and attacked the other, steeper hill out of the village with the gusto Julia brings to everything she does in life. She nearly made it, but the wheels started to spin and she ground to a halt. Rachael, the churchwarden, had been driving behind her. Her rugged four wheel drive could probably have overtaken Julia's car, but Rachael's nerve failed her at the critical moment and she pulled up. Next came Alf, the postman, who drove his van with quiet confidence at the hill. He didn't get as far as Rachael before he

stopped and slid slowly back down again. "Well that's it then," said Anna, the postmistress, "our village is cut off!"

While she was dispensing coffee to the slightly shaken drivers, there was the noise of crunching gears. A little red car appeared at the top of the steep hill and Ralph, the village's oldest inhabitant, slalomed down between the litter of abandoned vehicles. He passed us with a wave and a cackle and we hurried out to watch as he gunned his engine for Mrs Addington's hill. His car fishtailed violently as he tackled the slope, but he kept going, struck Mrs Addington's shiny bumper a glancing blow as he edged past it and continued triumphantly out of sight. It was time for his early lunchtime pint at the Friendly Ferret and no amount of snow was going to stop him. "Our village is nearly cut off," amended Anna.

For those of us marooned, a carnival mood prevailed. The rural day continued, with animals to be fed and businesses to be run, but there were certainly some snowballs thrown, too. The school bus hadn't reached the village, and happy bands of older children headed off with their sledges to The Bottom, a field that dives sharply down to a thick hedge, needing nerves of steel and preferably a suit of chain mail to negotiate successfully. Over Maurice's garden wall I could see his youngest daughter building a snow sheep on the lawn, complete with realistic pebble eyes. A thaw was forecast and our state of siege would not last long, but just for the time being the whole village relaxed and enjoyed the snow.

Chairman of the Board

Colin, my neighbour, looked into the long weeks of winter yet to come and decided that a village Scrabble tournament would be a nice idea. We could meet in each other's houses, play a time-honoured board game in a spirit of gentle competition and cheerfully while away the cold, dark days. Colin would organise the tournament, set the rules, extract a contribution from each team to donate towards the ravenous heating arrangements of our frozen stone church, and present a modest prize to the winning team. Modest, that is, unless he himself won the tournament, which would be an entirely different matter.

He pinned up a notice in the village shop outlining his plans and asking for entrants, and I examined it dubiously. I had uneasy childhood memories of rain lashing down on a seaside holiday cottage and an old Scrabble board being unearthed as the last refuge from boredom. But I admired Colin's stand against the winter blues and, alongside a heartening number of other villagers, signed my husband and myself up. Teams were to decide among themselves who would host each match, but only words found in the host's home dictionary would be allowed. We were to keep a record of points won and have fun: after all, "Scrabble is only a game".

It is indeed – gamesmanship started almost immediately. Colin hosted the vicar and his wife Joan for his first match and plied them with rich food and fine wine before ushering them through to the sitting room where the reverend fell asleep in the very comfortable armchair provided. He had to be nudged awake by Joan to make each move in the game that followed, and Colin's team won easily. Ben, who lives next door to Colin, noted the incident with interest. When his turn came to host Colin, he produced a mighty three volume dictionary – borrowed from an academic friend – and slowly looked up every word, no matter how simple, suggested by Colin's team. Colin found the endless delays so infuriating that he played at random and lost the game to Ben.

Greatly encouraged, Ben bought a tiny magnetic travelling Scrabble board before his game with Mr and Mrs Addington. Although the Addingtons' combined intellectual capacity is truly formidable, their combined eyesight is not the best. Their concentration drained away as they fiddled with the minuscule letters and Ben's team won again. Ben and Colin were

not the only Scrabble players of guile. Audrey, our venerable and intimidating garden queen, produced an ancient Scrabble board with so many letters missing that only she and her husband (who were used to its quirks) could form any meaningful words while using it. This stood her in excellent stead until the other teams wised up and insisted on inviting her back to their own homes and more reliable Scrabble sets.

As the season progressed, and tactics came under scrutiny, passions were awakened that, in a more spontaneous part of the world, would have resulted in piles of bleeding bodies. In our tranquil English village it merely meant that certain people said 'Good morning!' to each other a little more stiffly than usual. Psychological warfare was at its height: Colin was spreading a totally unfounded rumour that Ben played online Scrabble and had an unfair advantage, while Ben had obtained an antique dictionary that smelled strongly of mildew and contained almost no usable modern words, when the whole thing ground to a sudden halt.

Almost unnoticed by the key players, a shy couple called Quentin and Rosie, newcomers to the village, had been modestly and expertly winning every game they played. And they had worked up an unassailable lead. Colin grumpily stashed away the silver cup he had dreamed of being awarded and substituted a set of scented candles given him by a well-meaning aunt for Christmas, which he thought would do nicely for Quentin and Rosie as their prize.

But when time eventually healed the sting of defeat, he would realise that his tournament had triumphantly achieved its objectives. Village hospitality had been shown, Scrabble had been played, a useful sum had been donated towards the church's heating system and Spring was now just around the corner. Same again next year? I'm game.

Come Dancing

Rachael the churchwarden took her family to visit her granny for Christmas. An inspirational lady of a certain age, she loaded the visitors into her sports car and whizzed them off to her weekly salsa dance class, where a riotous evening ensued. Rachael returned home full of the joys of salsa, convinced that latino dancing was just what we all needed to shake off post-Christmas blues and meet the New Year with sparkling eyes and washboard stomachs.

Our village takes a measured approach to new concepts and greeted Rachael's suggestion with caution. I had a vague idea that salsa came in bowls to be handed round with nibbles at drinks parties, and my neighbours knew no better. Rachael chanced upon Frank and asked how he'd feel about taking up salsa. His actual comment was unprintable but his sentiment was clear.

Undaunted, Rachael continued her crusade to introduce salsa to the village by emphasising the warming qualities of dance as we grouped around the hot-water urn after a chilly church service, thawing our hands on mugs of tea. In the village shop she waxed lyrical on the merits of keeping fit within a framework of fun and safety, and in the bar of the Friendly Ferret, she described the pleasure to be gained by people moving together in synchronised harmony. "What's salsa like, then?" Frank's wife Phyllis asked. "Sort of shuffling backwards and forwards with a wiggle in the middle," Rachael said.

We mulled over the idea, and then her campaign got the boost it needed: Quentin and Rosie, newcomers who'd been quietly listening, confessed that they were seasoned salsa dancers and agreed to demonstrate the steps and help any villagers who might like to learn how to move in hot Cuban rhythms. Audrey, our gardening guru from the same generation as Rachael's granny, asked what would be the correct costume for salsa dancing. When told that a dress with a bit of movement would fit the bill, she promised to look out her Liberty-print shirtwaister. Before Quentin and Rosie could reconsider their offer, a poster appeared on the village notice board inviting everybody interested to attend an inaugural salsa demonstration and practice session, with themed eats. After much discussion, it was concluded that chilli con carne with fruit salad to follow would be suitably exotic, yet not too scary.

When the evening came around, almost everyone decided to have a go and I arrived in the village hall to a heartening bustle. Rachael inserted a CD into the sound system, which gave a startled crackle, then filled the air with a foot-tapping beat. The display commenced. Quentin and Rosie had been in the village for a year; several of us had sampled Quentin's homemade beer and met Rosie walking their Norfolk terrier, but these pleasant encounters had not prepared us for the couple that now bounded into our midst and began a sizzling dance routine. Frank had eyes like saucers. "Flippin' 'eck," he breathed reverently as he eyed Rosie's swaying hips and Quentin's manfully strutting figure. Seizing his wife, Frank trod heavily on her bunion and whirled her into the dance.

While he and Phyllis took to salsa like ducks to water, not all found it so easy. Mr Addington did his best, muttering "1-2-3-back-5-6-7" under his breath, but Mrs Addington was a solid lump of disapproval. Quentin went over: "It's all about moving the body, getting the ghetto pulse," he urged helpfully. Mrs Addington's body was firmly enclosed in tweed multi-layering and had no intention of pulsating, ghetto or otherwise. Quentin persevered: "Mrs Addington, could you wiggle your hips?" "No, I could not!" And that was that.

As the evening continued, our efforts could not compare with Quentin and Rosie's liquid ease of movement, but what we lacked in finesse we made up for in tenacity. The village hall heated to sauna temperature and we laughed, ate huge quantities of chilli and danced and laughed again until we finally returned home with Cuban rhythms still ringing in our ears. Rachael's campaign worked wonders and as a village we can now say a fervent: "Viva la salsa!" Except for Mrs Addington, that is, who much prefers her comforts cold.

Quentin's guide to first steps in salsa dancing

Rosie and I are newcomers to the village and we are keen to bond. So we were delighted to give a little exhibition of salsa dancing, because salsa is above all a social dance form. Quite honestly we found the villagers initially resistant. We wanted to demonstrate the soul of salsa dancing, the sensuous challenge and yield of the dance pattern, but at first they tended to giggle or go for second helpings at the buffet.

However we persevered and soon they joined in and some began to show real aptitude. Frank and Phyllis in particular were amazingly keen, though Frank has yet to develop finesse. We encouraged everybody to follow these simple steps, given for the leader:

- *Face your partner, hold her loosely (Frank!) around the waist with your right hand. Then take your partner's right hand in your left, while her left hand is on your right shoulder.*
- *On the first beat, step forward with your left foot, while your partner steps back with her right foot.*
- *On the second beat, step in place with your right foot, while your partner continues to mirror your movements.*
- *On the third beat step back with your left foot, on the fourth beat hold in place.*
- *On the fifth beat step back with your right foot, on the sixth beat step in place with your left foot.*
- *On the seventh beat step forward with your right foot, on the eighth hold in place with your left foot.*
- *Repeat.*

It was going so well that Rosie and I decided to add the authentic Cuban hip movement and that is when we had a problem with Mrs Addington. I attempted to instruct her in the proud yet urgent strut of the true salsa dancer, but she said it was disgusting and left for a brisk walk in the fresh air. We missed her of course, but I have to say that the dance flourished after her departure. Rosie took Mr Addington in hand and he improved remarkably quickly. Salsa music is very dynamic, and Colin kept the merlot flowing and eventually I felt that, as a community, we were experiencing the authentic throb of the ghetto. Which was quite something for a village hall in North Wiltshire, in January.

February

A Rustic Romance

In the early days of February, when snowdrops unfurl from the frozen earth, catkins shake their pollen from hazel trees and lovers' thoughts turn to candlelit suppers, our village is a bit of a slow starter. We've got snowdrops and catkins all right, gardens and hedgerows full of them, but to describe the seasonal mood as one of simmering romance would be misleading. Settled contentment, on the whole, would be nearer the mark.

Rachael the churchwarden, for example, bumped into her husband on the Countryside March when he trod on her foot with his wellington boot and it was love at first sight. Maurice the farmer met his wife on a hedge laying course and they have laid numerous hedges together since; and many years ago Jack turned to Phyllis, the pretty girl at the next desk in the village school, and said, "How about it?" One thing led to another, and there followed a simple wedding at our local church conducted by the now late lamented vicar 'Norman the Sermon', a good man but boring in the extreme. Their honeymoon was spent harvesting leeks for extra money with which to set up house, and they led a gentle country existence till his early death some years ago.

Although she mourned Jack sincerely, Phyllis had been courted assiduously by Frank since before I arrived in the village and the pair were probably the nearest we had to 'love's young dream'. For many years Frank was a commitment-phobe, unwilling to dip a toe into the uncharted waters of matrimony. Then one evening, as he sat in Phyllis's cottage eating her rabbit casserole, something mysterious and beautiful happened – Frank proposed and Phyllis accepted. Only now, Frank had a new problem to overcome, which he relayed to a fascinated circle of us in our local pub: Phyllis wanted to get married at the top of the Empire State Building, in New York.

Her first wedding had been lovely in its rural simplicity, but now she fancied something different and she thought that New York would fit the bill nicely. The trouble was that, apart from an annual pilgrimage to the Game Fair, Frank preferred to keep within a ten-mile radius of our village. He wanted to tie the knot in his familiar cold, stone church and not some city where, according to his admittedly basic research, giant gorillas swatted at planes. It was a step too far, even to please Phyllis.

There the matter stood for the star-crossed lovers until the traditional pancake party, held every year in the village hall, close enough to Valentine's Day for us to deck it out with hearts and subdued lighting. Conversation with Phyllis drifted towards the practicalities of an overseas wedding. Her friends and neighbours tried to work out an acceptable answer to the impasse. Perhaps another venue could be found that was still exciting, but closer to home? "How about the Clifton Suspension Bridge?" suggested Rachael. Those around the table agreed that the bridge was truly iconic.

The vicar intervened; he thought that the bishop might have an issue with the solemnisation of marriage on a hanging piece of architecture high above the River Avon. Holding the ceremony in a crop circle, or even at Stonehenge, was mooted and turned down on grounds of feasibility. Then Anna, our postmistress, had a brainwave, involving the genius of her friend Margaret who decorated cakes professionally. It was a compromise solution, but as she suggested it, Phyllis's eyes brightened and she looked fondly over to where Frank was gazing soulfully back at her over his pint of Old Ferret.

Frank and Phyllis's wedding in our church was a very happy occasion. The reception took place in the village hall, which we'd decorated to resemble the streets of New York as closely as our collective ingenuity and enormous amounts of backing paper and poster paint could muster. Pride of place went to the glorious cake, fashioned as a replica of the Empire State Building, with marzipan taxi cabs cruising around the base. It was certainly different and Phyllis beamed with delight as she and her new husband cut into its rich, fruity foundations, surrounded by their friends. Proof indeed that our village does have a romantic heart. It's just that, like the snowdrops, it lies well hidden.

A Fishy Business

I was standing in the village post office and shop on a miserable, wet day. The door swung open, with an aggressive jingle of the bell, and Mr Addington entered with his normal state of Righteous Indignation winched up to Total Outrage. "There's brawling in the open streets!" he exclaimed. Anna, Rachael and I exchanged bewildered glances. Sounds of battle drifted through the door that had been left ajar: "Get off my fish, you horrible man!" "You leave my drains alone!"

After a brief scuffle during which Rachael and Mr Addington got wedged together in the doorway to their mutual horror, we burst out to see an astounding sight. Julia, our local hedge-fund manager, was trying to grind her spike heel through the rigid leather boots of Frank. Frank, normally a benign and peaceful man, was wielding his billhook in a warlike fashion. They were screaming at each other from point-blank range.

Suddenly, a shoal of huge, multicoloured fish sailed down the roadside gully past our feet. They did a four-fin skid past the new metal grille over the drain, shot through the gap in the hedge, dived into the raging stream below and vanished. Julia burst into tears, and Frank downed his weapon. There was a sudden, appalled silence.

Anna hauled everyone out of the rain into the shop. As Julia recovered over a coffee, and Frank consoled himself with a bottle of his favourite ale, the sad story came out. Julia had a pond in her garden at the top of the hill. Not a pond of mud, slime and duckweed like mine. Hers was a miracle of Cotswold stone, wire herons and clean water in which enormous koi carp drifted. Then it rained, the water level rose and that morning, to her horror, she had looked out and seen that her pond had disappeared under a lake of flood water. The koi had also looked out and, realising that their world was beautiful but limited, opted to go for the Great Escape.

Meanwhile Frank was walking the lanes, clearing gullies and drains with his billhook, as he had done since he was a lad. Without Frank's unpaid ministrations the village would have disappeared under flood water many more times than it has. But after years of performing this service, Frank had developed a fierce, proprietary attachment to the village drains quite out of keeping with his normal diffident personality. The bridge by the shop had recently been strengthened and though the local council had made a nice job of it, the roadside gully had been diverted to drain through a shiny new metal grille. This did not please

Frank, who preferred the previous arrangement. That morning he had been happily diverting the rainwater back through the hedge with the aid of his billhook when he looked up and saw Julia as she raced down the hill and frantically started trying to force the water back to the grille, hoping to catch the koi on the metal bars before they slipped through. Mistaking her shouts of "koi! koi! koi!" for an ancient hedge-fund manager's war cry, and clocking the fact that she was meddling with his beloved drains, Frank went into defensive action.

Everything calmed down quickly after the Battle of the Drains. Frank returned to maintaining the village watercourses, to the benefit of all. Julia had her pond replaced with a water feature. Water now slides charmingly over slabs of Cotswold stone – no fish, but some lovely statues. The carp were never seen again. Julia harbours hopes that they were adopted by a fish-lover downstream, but I have my doubts. The heron that haunts the bridge is normally a catwalk size zero among birds. But when I saw him recently, he had a newly prosperous air. He flapped off up the stream like a 747 with full cargo and I think he knows exactly where the koi ended up.

A Flash in the Pan

One of the many nice things about our annual pancake race is that it takes place down the main street, which is in fact our only street. We go up the middle, past the village shop, round the mighty oak tree and finally collapse in an exhausted heap next to Maurice the farmer's silage clamp. The races are hard fought, and villagers are in training for days before the event. Julia, the hedge-fund manager, bought herself a lightweight 'racing' frying pan; gardening guru Audrey practised running with her terriers and could be seen in her garden with the dogs orbiting her at all points of the compass, attached to her by their flexi leads. Even the Addingtons marched to the village shop in perfect step, Mr Addington's right leg invisibly shackled to his wife's left one. They were determined to be in the running for the three-legged event.

On the big day, snow was forecast and an enormous black cloud hung over the village. This didn't seem to put anyone off and the main street was bustling with people, dogs and the Addingtons' cat Ming, who likes to be present at social gatherings. Dogs in the know keep well clear of her as she is a feline black belt in martial arts.

Studying the list of races, I noted with interest that this year the first one was for 'Veterans aged 80+'. Last year the veterans were deemed to be those over 75, but Audrey (who decided the categories) had just had an important birthday and didn't yet see herself as a veteran, so the age had been bumped up. No matter, our village contains plenty of feisty over-80s so I went across to watch them revving up for the start. Our oldest inhabitant, Ralph, took an early lead, combining ferocious pancake tossing from a cast-iron pan with sweeping movements of his walking stick, which cleared his way ahead. However, Maurice's mum

June shot away from the pack in her mobility scooter, frying pan busy, slalomed around Ralph with nonchalant ease and whizzed over the finish line as our first winner.

Next up was the popular 'Dogs and Owners' category. Dogs are everywhere in our village – grinning from gateways, walking their owners and generally joining in village life, but the pancake race, for them, is a golden day. Races involving pancake tossing? From a dog's point of view, it's a win-win situation. They careered off the starting line in an ecstasy of vocal joy, dragging their owners behind them. Audrey was going well, at the centre of a merry-go-round of yapping terriers, but Ben overtook her, his legs going like pistons and Bodger his Labrador galumphing along at his side. They were about to burst across the finish line in first place when Bodger spotted a dropped pancake at the side of the course and decided that it looked a better bet than the one in his master's frying pan. He galloped at right angles straight in front of his legs, Ben went crashing to the ground and Audrey won the race.

Although now officially walking wounded, nothing would deter Ben from watching the remaining events. He cheered on the proceedings from the sidelines with an unharmed Bodger sitting at his side, wolfing down his (second) pancake. The first flakes of snow began to fall as the last race, for 'Parent and Offspring', was about to start. As the participants rushed across the line I could see June accelerating her scooter, with Maurice pounding beside her in his wellies, but they were no match for my next-door neighbour Kay who ran with her 12-year-old son, both built like greyhounds and going all out for gold.

I stood by Ben as the whole pack ran past at full speed, multi-coloured aprons fluttering, frying pans flailing and attendant dogs barking. The snow settled on Ben's battered chef's hat as we watched them disappear into the gathering blizzard. "Mad as a box of frogs," said Ben with satisfaction. "Aren't they great?"

All Stitched Up

Back in the dark days before Christmas, I had a visit from my next-door neighbour Kay. This time it wasn't to borrow a cup of something or enlist my help rounding up the livestock that constantly flowed through her colander-like fences. She was on a recruiting drive for the knitting club. "Oh come on, Aly," she said, "everyone will be there. Mrs Addington will be there and, well, everyone. Knitting is really fashionable nowadays – you'll love it." Then to hammer home her point she produced a knitting pattern. "Look, we're starting with Joan's pattern for a tea cosy from the 1950s. Isn't it cool?" I couldn't imagine anything less cool than knitting a tea cosy in the company of Mrs Addington and other assorted village elders, but I'll try anything once.

The knitting club met in the vicarage, a modest house in the village where the vicar and his wife Joan welcomed all comers with true saintliness. After several make-overs, the Old Rectory had every possible convenience, but Joan sometimes talked of the days when she lived there, when cold, damp flagstones covered the downstairs floors and water only flowed reliably from one tiny tap in the cellar.

The modern vicarage was warm and cosy and several villagers were gathered there when I entered. As I tried to dredge up early memories of how to cast-on, advice came from all sides, and after a while I was successfully launched on the first rows of my tea cosy and able to look around. Joan was twirling her knitting needles professionally and already had a small pile of completed cosies by her side, ready to distribute as Christmas presents. Kay had continually misread the pattern, and her tea cosy had formed into a long cone. Mrs Addington was knitting with organic undyed handspun wool that resembled long strands of porridge. She worked with such concentration that she didn't even look up when Julia discovered with a shriek that she'd knitted her tea cosy into the cashmere cardigan she was wearing, and the two were inextricably linked.

Kay was right: I grew to love the club. After a few sessions, the knitting became easier, and I was ridiculously proud of my finished tea cosy. Christmas came and went and, during the gloomiest part of the year, the knitting club met regularly and flourished. Funnily enough, Mrs Addington, normally grimly effective at everything she did, had not really taken to knitting. Now, while Joan knitted a complicated lacy jumper, Anna the postmistress tackled a colourful tank top, and even I was getting on well with some fingerless mittens, Mrs Addington was only just finishing off her tea cosy with a tightly wound organic pom-pom. "That will look lovely on your teapot," Joan said, encouragingly. "Mr Addington and I do not take tea," snapped back Mrs Addington, looking down thoughtfully at her handiwork.

A few days later I was in the village shop when Mr Addington entered and glared at Anna. "I regret to note that you have no sun-dried tomato paste," he stated belligerently. The weather was bitterly cold and Mr Addington's thin hair was covered by a most distinctive bobble hat. I sneaked a look at it. The holes for spout and handle had been firmly sewn shut, but I recognised it at once. "I like your hat, Mr Addington," I said, daringly. "It was a present from my dear wife," he said, thawing momentarily before returning to the attack. "And, Anna, I grieve to see that you stock no passata, despite my repeated requests." Anna smiled at him. "The passata is over there, Mr Addington. Next to the sun-dried tomato paste."

When he had left, still grumpy despite an armful of quality tomato-based products, I grinned at Anna. There is no doubt that it is far easier to deal cheerfully with a difficult customer when you know (and he doesn't) that he's wearing a porridge-coloured tea cosy on his head.

Joan's knitting pattern for a very useful tea cosy

I was given this knitting pattern by my dear Mama. She was such an elegant lady and I remember so well that she loved to drink Earl Grey tea out of fine bone china tea cups. She always used a silver teapot, and on it she would invariably place a tea cosy knitted with her own hands in the colours of our local football team. Hot pink and orange for the Chortlebury Wanderers – it really lit up the tea tray!

Tea cosy (ribbed):

Abbreviations: k: knit, p: purl, ktbl: k2 together through back of loops.

Use 5mm knitting needles and either aran yarn or two strands of double knitting yarn held together.

Cast on 53 stitches.
*K2, p2, repeat from * to last stitch, k1.
Repeat till work measures 18cm.
K2 (p3 together k1) 12 times, p2, k1 (29 stitches).
K2, p2 (k1, p1) 12 times, k1.
K1 (ktbl) 12 times, k2 together (16 stitches).
K1, p to last stitch, k1.
K2 together 8 times across row (8 stitches).

Break yarn, thread through remaining stitches, pull together tightly.

Knit up another piece exactly the same.

Sew up seams with spout and handle holes in appropriate places. Add pom-pom on top.

Pom-pom:

1. Cut out two doughnut shapes from stiff cardboard. I draw around the bottom of a mug for the outside circle and then around a spice jar for the inside circle.

2. Place the two cardboard doughnuts together and wrap yarn evenly around the cardboard cutouts, pushing it through the middle of the doughnut with every wrap.

3. When you have wrapped plenty of wool around the doughnuts, use small, sharp scissors to cut your way along the edge of the cardboard doughnut. When you are all the way around, pull the cardboard gently apart and wrap a length of wool tightly around the middle. Knot it securely and leave long end dangling.

4. Pull the two pieces of cardboard carefully away, then fluff up your pom-pom and sew it securely onto the top of the tea cosy using the long end.

March

The Good Shepherd

I gazed thoughtfully at my in-lamb ewes, who looked like over-inflated woolly rugby balls. Lambing time was approaching, but was I ready? I had read a pile of sheep care books, watched my way through some blood-curdling videos and bought a T-shirt saying 'Happy Birthday to Ewe!' to wear for the births, but was it enough? Even though I had the moral support of Frank, the sheep expert who lived down the lane, I knew that it wasn't. If I wanted to give my girls the best up-to-the-minute maternity support, I needed to back up the theory with some practical. I signed up for the lambing techniques course at the local agricultural college.

I arrived at the classroom and had a cautious look around. The lecturer looked knowledgeably competent. So did my fellow students. Even the fake ewe we would practise on looked knowledgeably competent. Things didn't improve when we sat round the table and introduced our sheep to each other. Bob had 2,000; Kathy had 600; Pauline had 19 ("nice little hobby flock, Pauline"); and I had three. With names. Yet what they lack in numbers, my girls make up for in character. Cue Teazle, character actress at the village nativity play and possibly the only sheep in the country who can shake hands. Then there's Foxy, obsessively fascinated with wheels of all sizes. And Dinky, chief sheep and polo mint addict.

We had been given a list of equipment to bring along. It's a bit like being told at antenatal class what to pack for the delivery suite. Perhaps less in the way of moisturiser and babygros, and more in the way of rubber gloves and powdered colostrum, but the same basic idea. Lubricant (tick), iodine (tick), lambing rope (oh yes). I had been particularly pleased with my pink lambing rope. I loved the fact that it could be authentic and yet bubble-gum pink. Now, set alongside everybody else's sober black lambing ropes, all it needed was to be printed with William Morris florals to mark me out as the complete amateur.

Still, it was a great course and by the end of the weekend I felt well prepared and raring to go. Dinky was the first away. Well before her due date she trotted up proudly one morning accompanied by two tiny lambs, the size and colour of Yorkshire terriers. She didn't need lambing ropes, of any shade. All that was left for me to do was bring the new family into the prepared stable, where the lambs flourished and Dinky lounged about guzzling hay and shouting rude remarks at the others.

After hours of sitting on a straw bale watching Dinky's twins pretending to be jumping beans, and Teazle and Foxy not having lambs, I headed home for a coffee. There was a tap on the back door. It was Frank, font of all country knowledge. "That little brown yow of yours has started. I hopped over the gate to see how she was doing, but she didn't need me. Thought you'd like to know!" he reported and vanished into the night. Help! Trailing lambing aids I hurtled down the field to the stable, but I was too late. Teazle hadn't just started – she'd finished. She looked up smugly from her tiny chocolate-coloured lamb and went back to licking him and telling him that he was the most talented baby ever born. As he staggered confidently over to feed, I hovered around helpfully. But Teazle knew, and her gorgeous newborn lamb knew, and I knew that they didn't really need me at all.

Surely Foxy would want my new-found skill? Foxy the airhead, whose only interest to date has been finding and then climbing onto wheels. Nope. She delivered her twins with brisk efficiency, and turned overnight into a practical and devoted mother (while retaining a strong interest in wheels).

After everybody's lambing was over, we had a course reunion in the local pub. Bob had some stirring tales to tell about the unstoppable conveyor belt of his commercial operation. Kathy shared some interesting experiences of delivering triplets. All I could contribute was a blown-up photograph of my twin lambs sitting together in a bucket, looking cute. Later that night I went down to say goodnight to my sheep. The stable scene in the dim light looked as woolly and appealing as the soft toy section of a top-class toy store. I sat down and let the lambs climb on me, while their yummy mummies watched with maternal pride, and realised that actually my little flock and I had done OK together.

Bookish Behaviour

Our village book club evolved over the years into a delightful ritual. We took it in turns to host it, and pick the book to be discussed. On the arranged evening, we chatted over a glass of wine, enjoyed dinner, and submitted the chosen book to a brief discussion over coffee and chocolates before returning home well satisfied. In terms of book choices, Rachael (our churchwarden) stipulated a happy ending, Anna (our postmistress) was adamant that nothing really nasty should happen, and I preferred an amusing style of writing. Other members went along happily with these criteria. Our club wasn't intellectually rigorous, but it was as pleasurably soothing as putting on a pair of alpaca socks inside one's wellies.

That was until the fateful day that Mrs Addington entered the post office as I was discussing the next book choice with Anna. On hearing the words 'book club', she stiffened like a pointer. "I didn't know the village had one. How marvellous! I would very much like to join." Anna and I looked at each other in consternation. It was highly likely that Mrs Addington would demand more of a book club than a feel-good factor. Still, it was her village too and we invited her to the next meeting.

This took place at Rachael's house, and true to form she had plumped for a book with a dayglo pink cover in which a happy ending was a cast-iron certainty. Mrs Addington arrived brandishing a well thumbed copy bristling with post-it notes. Rachael got flustered and offered her a glass of chardonnay, forgetting Mrs Addington was stridently teetotal. Waving the bottle aside, her jaw jutting with literary zeal, Mrs Addington got straight down to business. In her view, the book was trite, a pastiche, but she felt some passages could be used as a vehicle for argument.

Something alien and uncomfortable had landed in our cosy little circle. Over supper, Mrs Addington looked around the table. "I notice no men are present," she reproached. "Mr Addington would very much like to be part of a more inclusive group, and I am sure Colin and the vicar would also enjoy the opportunity for a really rigorous discussion. In fact Mr Addington has already compiled a comprehensive list of books he thought would be ideal for future meetings." A short, appalled silence followed.

And, inevitably, the next meeting took place at the Addingtons' house. I turned up in good time, but Colin and the vicar were there already, discussing the chosen book – "a bleak portrait of repressed American family life". Cranberry juice was served, then came a short break for a wholesome meal, after which in-depth examination of various marked-up chapters continued. Several of us couldn't join in because, repelled by the worrying graphics on the front cover and the printed list of questions for discussion, we hadn't actually read it. And from what we could pick up, it fulfilled absolutely none of our previous favourite criteria. The characters that lived uneasily inside its pages all seemed determined to avoid a happy ending by any means possible. Nasty things happened throughout, and it most definitely wasn't funny.

However, while some of us sat there wondering how soon we could go home, the Addingtons, Colin and the vicar were having the time of their lives hammering away at the literary merits of the book. I even detected signs of interest being shown by some of the more serious minded members of our old book club. And this was how our village ended up with Book Club Heavy and Book Club Lite. This month, Book Club Heavy is studying a searing exposé of Stasi collaboration, with every symptom of keen enjoyment. Meanwhile Book Club Lite will immerse itself in the pleasant daily lives of some Edinburgh citizens. After dinner. For a short time. And no prizes for guessing which of the two clubs I belong to!

Village Vigilantes

It's not always easy being the husband of a high-achieving hedge fund manager, so when Julia's husband Matt has one of his ideas for the empowerment of our community, we tend to humour him. This time he decided that the village needed a Neighbourhood Watch scheme.

Our neighbourhood watching to date had been of the informal variety. Newcomers to the village would come under the steady gaze of the locals. This was not aggressive, but details would be remembered if needed. And it wasn't only outsiders who were observed. One gusty morning I staggered outside with a heavy load of washing and hung it on my rotary clothes line. The sheets billowed out like sails, then the line keeled over and collapsed into the mud. The geese hurried over for a good rummage, and the whole situation was less than ideal.

I felt in need of some consoling chocolate so set off for the village shop. Mr Addington passed me. "Damn shame about your washing," he said. In the shop, Anna the postmistress was in sympathetic mode: "Aly, your lovely white sheets! I heard all about it!" Back outside and eating my chocolate I found that Frank, my neighbour, was loitering with advice. "You should string a line between your apple trees with a nice piece of hazel to hold it up," he said without preamble: "I don't hold with them rotary driers. Doubt you do now, neither!" When I got home, the phone was ringing. It was Rachael the churchwarden. "Your geese are a scream," she said. "They were having a tug-of-war with one of your pillowcases when I drove past." There was no doubt about it – our neighbourhood was already being watched. Very effectively.

Still, Matt was keen, and the village supported his plans. We shivered in the stone-cold church while a Police Community Support Officer told us we should mark everything that couldn't be nailed down and train CCTV cameras on everything that could be. We bought striking blue and white signs to display around the village. Matt issued us with notebooks in which we should write down incidents, and a telephone flow chart to alert neighbours once the incidents had been noted. We were ready for anything.

There were some false alarms: the powerful black car that suddenly appeared outside the church and remained for several days looking ominously like a getaway car was traced through police computers to Rachael's granny, who was on a week's visit. But then came a phone call from Matt: "Kay's just rung – somebody has siphoned off her heating oil!" and the Neighbourhood Watch machine swung into action. We assembled in the church to decide on a course of action and agreed to take it in turns to monitor the main route into the village. How would we identify a potential oil thief? He would be carrying buckets and a hosepipe and would be smelling strongly of diesel – also a fair description of Maurice, the local farmer, after an altercation with his tractor. "Use your common sense," said Matt, "you'll know a criminal if you see one."

My husband and I had been assigned the dawn patrol and at the appointed hour we drove to the village green. Dawn is not usually my favourite time of day, but this was wonderful: owls swooped, foxes slunk, badgers bustled and, as day broke, the air pulsated with bird song. The only sign of human life we saw was Frank, setting off to feed his sheep. This was also the sign our watch was over so we returned home.

Ours turned out to be the last night watch. Kay called later and apologetically admitted that her oil hadn't been stolen – she'd forgotten to order more. The culprit was absent-mindedness, rather than rural crime. Still, as Matt said, the exercise had been a valuable dress rehearsal. We were now vigilant as a community. If someone carrying buckets and a hosepipe and smelling strongly of diesel (apart from Maurice) appeared in the village we would be ready for them. Actually we always were – but now it is official.

Birds of a Feather

The other day I was leaning against a dry-stone wall, gazing at our pleasant landscape of rounded hills and stone cottages. A distant wisp of smoke rose from where Maurice, the farmer, was hedge laying and one of the sheep I was watching, after careful consideration, ate a primrose. The scene seemed timeless, and yet it would be a mistake to think that nothing changes around here. In fact, there's been nothing short of a coup (or should that be coop?) in poultry management, for example.

When I first arrived, life wasn't much fun for village fowl. My neighbour Frank's chicken run was a typical example of its kind: a dreary selection of brown birds, stinging nettles and a pile of old scrap. The hens laid their eggs and, when they stopped, went into the roasting tin. I found them a depressing sight but Frank, in turn, was horrified when I fell for the puffball charms of Pekin bantams and brought home a colourful flock to potter around my garden. "What's the use of them?" he asked me, looking at their small stature and almost complete lack of egg-laying ability. How could I explain that I wasn't going to eat my hens? My little crew were there as friends, amusement and therapy – the crooning of a happy batch of bantams settling on their perches for the night is the most comforting noise. Frank and I had to agree to differ on the chicken subject.

I wasn't alone in considering them as more than a mere food source, and a new wave of poultry arrived in the village – arrayed in spots, frills and pom-poms, and living in painted pagodas and edgy techno-domes rather than the corrugated-iron shacks that used to be considered more than adequate. Rachael, the churchwarden, invited me along as moral support on a hen-buying expedition. We arrived at a spotless yard surrounded by cages of immaculate chickens of every variety. Rachael took her pick and paid in a shop stocked with arks, books and food supplements, all of which seemed vital to the future wellbeing of her new flock. By the time we had loaded up

the car it was obvious that, no matter how many eggs they laid, Rachael's Welsummers would never turn a profit. They could, however, introduce her little daughters to the simple joys of egg collecting. It was just a new way of looking at things.

Mr and Mrs Addington, predictably, hold the moral high ground among local poultry enthusiasts, ever since Mr Addington arrived home triumphantly with a box of semi-naked, rescued battery hens. These were ushered ceremoniously into luxury quarters and, after several weeks of pampering, rewarded their saviours with glossy new feathers and started laying again out of sheer gratitude.

The old and new regime clashed recently when I was chatting over the garden gate to Julia, the hedge fund manager. Julia's hens are a breed called Cotswold Legbar, who dress in a feathery melange of pastel tones and lay eggs in sophisticated shades of aqua, olive and taupe. We were soon joined by Frank, ambling past on his way to the village shop, and also by Mirabelle, the dowager of Julia's flock, who strolled over and gazed up at us. "You'll have to boil that old girl a good long time to make decent eating," observed Frank matter-of-factly. Julia stiffened, picked Mirabelle up and clapped her hands over the place where Mirabelle presumably kept her ears. "That was highly inappropriate!" she snapped and stalked off with Mirabelle under one arm, leaving Frank dumbfounded.

Actually Frank doesn't keep hens himself any more. His new wife Phyllis prefers gourmet chicken goujons from the local farm shop to the scraggy old boilers Frank used to produce. And the poultry of this parish are more than happy to leave the whole area of chicken husbandry to the professionals and enjoy their new status as a leisure pursuit. For hens at least, life in this village has changed out of all recognition. You might even say they've reached the top of the pecking order.

Mrs Addington's favourite hen breeds

Wallace and I adhere to a macrobiotic diet and shun all poultry products, especially the extreme yang of an egg. However I consider hens to be pleasing companions and their produce is always acceptable to our omnivorous neighbours. I feel it is my moral duty to assist hens in reduced circumstances so the majority of my flock have been rescued from batteries, but Wallace and I sometimes obtain pure bred poultry to mark a special occasion. Here is a list of my personal preferences:

Sussex. An amiable bird that lays a great many eggs. I am particularly fond of the Light Sussex, which is white with black feathers around the neck and tail, while Wallace prefers the Speckled Sussex. I would call the Sussex a good beginner's hen.

Marans. We have Cuckoo Marans which are speckled like cuckoos, a most attractive colouration. They tend to be friendly hens and lay mahogany brown eggs.

Orpington. Big, feathery birds with a most delightful nature. Pantaloon, my favourite Orpington hen, is Buff in colour. Despite her bulk, her eggs are modest in size and she is an excellent mother.

Silkie. If a broody hen is desired, you could not do better than to acquire the services of a silkie. Silkies have soft, silky feathers and blue earlobes, which I consider to be rather fetching. They are calm birds who exhibit a high standard of maternal responsibility.

Pekin. Were I to select a primus inter pares, a chicken which 'does it for me' even more than the rest (I think that would be an acceptable modern translation) I would unhesitatingly select the Pekin bantam. We obtained a pair of Lavender Pekins to mark a visit to Beijing and they have given constant joy. In shape they are small and rotund with feathered feet. Admittedly they are not prolific egg layers, not a source of concern for Wallace and myself but they accompany me when I am weeding my garden and do not scratch in the flower beds. I recommend them highly.

April

Art and Soul

In his distant, fiery youth, and after drinking several pints of Old Ferret with his mates in the Friendly Ferret, my neighbour Frank heaved a brick through the stained glass depiction of Noah's Ark in the best window in our village church. He scored a direct hit on the dove. Frank was very sorry about it afterwards, but the result was Noah holding up an increasingly ancient mass of sticky tape instead of the biblical symbol. The wind whistled through the gaps in the tape and made the church even colder. We fought the chill with tiny hot air blasters that heated our feet to boiling point while we froze from the ankles up.

Julia, our local hedge fund manager, shivered through one service too many and (being Julia) called a committee meeting. Our village divides into those who enjoy being on a committee (anything for a laugh) and make up the bulk of the Parish Council, Friends of the Village Hall, etc, and those who would rather have root canal treatment without anaesthetic. It was the former set that assembled around Julia's distressed pine table in her gracious farmhouse kitchen, while she steered us competently through the turbulent waters of Health & Safety issues, both real and perceived, towards the lighthouse of fundraising to improve our church.

She guided us away from a pet show, a carnival with floats and (Frank's suggestion) a sponsored competition to see who could get furthest up the rotten wooden stairs that spiralled up the church tower without falling through the treads. We decided to hold an art exhibition in the church. Julia's husband, Matt, attended the next meeting. "We need something conceptual," he growled. There was a startled pause. Anna, the postmistress, said that her friend Una did very pretty flower paintings, but this obviously wasn't what Matt meant. He undid a portfolio and produced an enormous black and white photograph of a gaunt woman seated in an attitude of despair underneath a motorway flyover. Colin, a serial committee member, cleared his throat. "Um, have you got anything that might be a bit more relevant to our village? Gardens or kittens, perhaps …?" Matt, with a furious scowl, silently left the room and did not return.

It turned out that the village could fill an art exhibition pretty comprehensively. Una's watercolour flowers were about as far from conceptual art as it was possible to get, but would probably sell well. Colin's wife, Bridget, went on artistic holidays in the Pyrenees, where she drew wise old faces in painstaking detail. Anna produced greetings cards out of handmade paper, while Frank revealed that he made napkin rings. Then there was an enthusiastic and unevenly talented village Art Group which would be delighted to have a showcase for their efforts. We were in business. All that remained was to pick a date, arrange the stewarding and settle down to a campaign of saturation advertising.

Exhibition Day dawned auspiciously. Spring sun shone down through Noah's Ark and ameliorated some of the chill caused by the surrounding mountains of unheated ecclesiastical

Cotswold stone. A friend of Julia's tinkled away on a celtic harp, although her music could barely be heard above the roar of the heaters ring-fencing her to prevent her fingers freezing to the strings. The visitors came in gratifyingly large numbers to drink a complimentary glass of wine (Anna's idea) and marvel at the exhibits.

Frank's napkin rings turned out to be old forks which he had tortured into circles with his welding kit. Some friends of Matt and Julia's wandered round the exhibition without much interest until they stopped admiringly by the unhappy forks. "Oh yes! So edgy!" They bought the lot, to use as place setting holders at their edgy dinner parties.

We voted to put Frank's contribution towards the cost of repairing the stained glass window, which seemed appropriate. He mounted a campaign to have Noah depicted holding a napkin ring aloft to celebrate the source of funding, but common sense prevailed. Full central heating may still be a twinkle in Julia's eye, but now we have some more efficient heaters and the stained glass dove of peace has finally returned to our church.

Animal Magic

Spring was in the air, and the sap was rising in our village. I waved to my neighbour Frank as he trundled past in his battered Land Rover, off to fetch his new wife Phyllis from a WI meeting. Heading in the other direction I saw Kipper the pub cat gliding along the hedgerow. Kipper was a muscular tom, the size and colour of a Scottish wildcat, whose affable nature and bursts of song made him as popular at the Friendly Ferret as Ed the publican, and for much the same reasons. I wished him well in his quest and went to answer the phone.

It was Rachael the church warden. "I've got duck chicks," she said vaguely. "What should I do?" I hurried around to her home, where she, her new baby and her small daughter Tabby were standing on the front lawn in the company of a fat white duck and a long line of adorable ducklings. None of those assembled seemed to have a clue what to do next. Living in a very rural spot is a constant delight, but predators enjoy it here, too. We have our share of foxes, mink and sparrow hawks, any one of which would have been delighted with a duckling dinner. After a swift check around Rachael's garden, we decided on the greenhouse as the safest place for the new family to set up home. Rachael and Tabby promised to take them on many accompanied outings to the pond and I left them satisfied that the new family would grow up safe and warm.

I continued to the village shop where Mr Addington was telling Anna, the postmistress, that his wife's Siamese cat Ming had finally fallen for the charms of their chosen Siamese stud cat, Bodacious Prince of Sapphires. After several visits to the Siamese stud in Derbyshire, where Ming had apparently explained very clearly that though Prince was a great guy, the chemistry just wasn't there, she now appeared to be expecting a happy event. Mr Addington was not a man given to displays of emotion, but his moustache twitched, and he definitely left the shop with a spring in his step. I strolled on to my field, to pamper my sheep who were in the later stages of pregnancy and were feeling hormonal and high maintenance.

Some weeks passed, during which I was fully occupied dealing with the many happy events at our stone cottage. The lambs duly arrived, my Pekin bantams hatched out their speckled fluff-ball chicks, and the gander was even nastier than usual to anybody who came near the shed where his geese communally brooded a mound of large white eggs. Occasionally I passed the Addingtons' house and noticed Ming sunning herself on the front doorstep. Mr Addington had obviously been correct in his prognosis, she was so full of kittens that she looked like a plump, cream-coloured butternut squash. He flagged me down one day when I was bounding around the village on Jigsaw, my black-and-white cob. "Ming has successfully delivered seven kittens!" he informed me and I promised I would come soon to admire the blue-blooded kittens.

I visited the Addington household the next day, with a bunch of flowers from the garden for Mrs Addington and a tin of tuna for Ming. I was ushered into the garden room, where Mrs Addington hung possessively over a miniature four poster bed from the depths of which Ming regarded me with maternal smugness. I gazed down speechlessly at what appeared to be a litter of Scottish wildcat kittens. "Of course Siamese colours don't come through properly for a while," Mr Addington said defensively, as the stripy little bundles squirmed and sucked.

I finally found my voice, "They're beautiful!" I exclaimed. But what I knew (and what everybody else present would realise once they were out of denial) is that where Bodacious Prince of Sapphires had failed, Kipper the pub cat had definitely succeeded.

Grapevine Gossip

My next-door neighbour, Kay, holidayed in Brittany and returned home via a French hypermarket. Confronted by apparently infinite choice, she panicked and brought back crates of tooth-enamel-dissolvingly awful wine, which she then distributed lavishly about the community. Many of us encountered Kay's selection at supper parties, as raffle prizes, or via the tombola and the commonly held view was that if it merely gave you an instant crushing headache, you had got off lightly.

Not that the village wine standards are high – Rachael the churchwarden likes pink wine; I go for ones with jokey names (a drop of Big Plonker, anyone?), while Maurice the farmer buys anything on special offer under £5. Colin is the exception, a connoisseur with a well stocked cellar, and he decided something had to be done. "I know people in the trade," he offered, "I'll organise a wine tasting."

And he was as good as his word. He named a date, lined up a friend who dealt in wine and opened his doors to anyone who wished to come along. To everyone's surprise this included Mr Addington, a staunch teetotaller – apparently Mrs Addington was at a macrobiotic seminar and he was keen to sample the alcohol-free wines that Julian, the rep, had promised to bring along. We settled down, eyed the forest of bottles that awaited us, alongside a large plastic bucket, and listened with interest to Julian's talk.

We learned about sniffing, swirling, and looking for the 'legs' – oily droplets that slide down the glass and tell the initiated what to expect – and the importance of jettisoning wine into the bucket, rather than gulping it down. In a spirit of solidarity we started with the alcohol-free wine, Julian taking the lead; "This is strange: I was expecting florals, but I'm getting

something much richer, mushroomy, almost farmyardy..." Maurice the farmer looked guiltily at Colin, "Um, I've been spreading manure in the next door field today. Perhaps if we shut the window?" Julian went into the kitchen to clear his tubes and we launched into a bottle of Chardonnay.

While most of us followed Julian's example and stuck noses into our glasses, Colin's next-door neighbour, Ben, who is never to be trusted, secretly swapped wines with Mr Addington. As we sniffed, swirled and occasionally spat into the bucket, the noise level rose. And it was noticeable that much of the noise came from Mr Addington. He was having a grand time, with Ben discreetly topping his glass up ("Best tonic wine I've ever tasted!"). At a gap in the proceedings, while we wrote down our impressions of the latest wine, Mr Addington gazed round lovingly at the assembled company: "Great village, best in the world," he said, and forming his sheet of tasting notes into a paper dart, he lobbed it into the bucket. We moved onto reds, and Mr Addington became belligerent. "The village grit bins should be green!" he shouted. "Why are they yellow? It's a horrible colour." And he glared defiantly at his startled neighbours. Ben gave him a large glass of Merlot. "Have some blackcurrant juice," he soothed. "Look for the legs in that." It worked. Mr Addington found his legs then lost them and sat back on the sofa. "The entire village should be street lit, it would be much safer!" he wailed, "but nobody listens to me!" and he sobbed into a large handkerchief.

We tried briefly to cheer him up, but the wines were excellent, we were being less than conscientious about the bucket and the party continued as Mr Addington fell into a deep sleep. We worked our way through the dessert wines then Julian, a consummate professional, eased out his order book and the tasting session was over. Mr Addington was nudged awake in time to place a large order for alcohol-free wine as a welcome home present for Mrs Addington and stumble muzzily away arm-in-arm with Ben.

Despite Colin's heroic attempts to educate our collective palate, and Julian's full order book, I can report only limited success. On the plus side, Kay's well of hypermarket plonk has finally run dry but Rachael still likes pink wine, although now she calls it 'rosé; I remain a sucker for a funny label and I can't see Maurice passing up a bargain. And Mr Addington, although revelling in his new friendship with Ben, remains a committed teetotaller.

A Floral Fiasco

At mercifully infrequent intervals we have a Spring Flower Festival in the church, organised with terrifying zeal by Audrey. Audrey can remember the time when our village was famous for its flower arranging. People would flock to the festival from miles around, and admiring articles were written in the local paper. Today, the expert flower arrangers of the village have mainly moved away, or passed away, and she is left with a group of bungling amateurs. Such as me.

Audrey felt the time was ripe to have another crack at the festival, and called a meeting in the church. "I thought the theme this year could be 'Blockbusters'," she announced. "I shall try my hand at The Sound of Music," she added firmly, getting her bid in first. Then she gave us an inspiring little talk, reminding us of the importance of impact, of making a statement with our flowers, and leaving room for an amusing twist. If I could just bag Jurassic Park, I was sure I could make a significant statement with some rhubarb leaves and a rubber velociraptor. Some hope! Audrey fixed me with a piercing eye: "Aly, I think you could take on Breakfast at Tiffany's." And that was that.

I trailed back home and looked at my garden. Did Constance Spry, at the height of her flower-arranging powers, have two solid Labradors whose funny five minutes every morning took them on a bulldozing trail of joy straight through the flower beds? I doubted it. Or hens who made surreptitious dust baths wherever tender seedlings were planted? Probably not.

Still, on Flower Festival morning, I gathered together the best blooms I could find on the kitchen table. Years ago at school I did 'Flower Arranging' for my Duke of Edinburgh Bronze Award and the basics remained with me: make a rough triangle with the A team of flowers, scatter the B team about harmoniously, and fill in the gaps with leaves. I was fairly pleased with my resulting floral poem to Breakfast at Tiffany's, and my amusing twist was that I arranged it in a teacup.

I carried it carefully over to the church. Churchwarden Rachael was surreptitiously stuffing a supermarket bouquet into a jug on a windowsill close to mine, while keeping a weather eye on Audrey's royal progress of inspection around the church. She had been assigned Finding Nemo, and hung a small plastic fish off a stalk before fading unobtrusively out of a side door just before Audrey reached us. Audrey eyed Rachael's contribution, and

my little teacup arrangement, said, "Ah, yes…" in a pained tone of voice and headed back towards the altar, her comfort zone. Here hedge fund manager Julia was creating a glorious white pedestal arrangement to represent Titanic on one side, and Joan the vicar's wife was shaping a wonderful Towering Inferno of red and orange blooms on the other side. Audrey relaxed visibly.

The doors were opened for visitors at 2pm. The crowd outside was quite respectable for a Flower Festival in a small, cold country church. We stood by our arrangements as Audrey clapped her hands for silence, and explained that everybody was encouraged to work out which blockbuster was represented by each arrangement and fill in a form accordingly. And this was when my flower arrangement made the impact she had asked for, though not quite in the manner intended. I had forgotten to tether my teacup to the window-catch, and it had been working its way unnoticed down the slope. As Audrey paid smiling tribute to her team of flower arrangers, my attempt at Breakfast at Tiffany's finally reached the edge of the windowsill, leaped into the void, and shattered explosively on the stone floor below.

Into the shocked silence that followed the crash came a single voice. "Well," said Ben, the village joker, busily filling in his form, "I'm putting Aly's flowers down as Gone with the Wind."

Audrey's instructions for a pedestal arrangement

First of all I want to make it absolutely clear that apart from myself we have only two talented flower arrangers in the village: Joan and Julia. I would entrust the altar pedestal arrangement to either lady without a moment's unease. However, if invited to instruct a less gifted villager in the art of arranging a pedestal, I would issue directions as follows:

1. Soak 'floral foam' (water-retaining sponge block) in a large bucket of fresh water. Allow it to fill with water then remove and drain. I find it hard to believe that anybody remains ignorant about the importance of correctly conditioned floral foam,

2. Strap foam in your chosen bowl (green floral tape is perfect for this), ensuring there is a gap to allow daily topping up with water, then secure bowl firmly to pedestal stand. If the pedestal arrangement were to topple over during a service it would startle the vicar and I would be personally mortified.

3. Gather together your foliage and flowers, which will of course have been properly prepared and left standing in water overnight. For an April arrangement your resources could include: Aquilegia, ceanothus, euonymus (on second thoughts, given the circumstances, I'll use everyday names), beech, catkin, daffodil, honeysuckle, hyacinth, iris, lilac, pussy willow, rosemary, solomon's seal, tulip. Just go outside and see what you can find. These are lovely materials and it would be hard to go wrong with them, even if florally challenged.

4. Mark a basic triangle with significant branches of foliage. Then bring more foliage out in front of the arrangement, by about a third of its height. Fill in the triangle with foliage then insert flowers. Buds on the outside, heavier and darker blooms down the middle. Group your colours attractively and I like to include a harmonious floral curve along the vertical and horizontal lines of my pedestal arrangement.

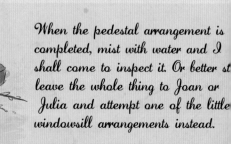

When the pedestal arrangement is completed, mist with water and I shall come to inspect it. Or better still leave the whole thing to Joan or Julia and attempt one of the little windowsill arrangements instead.

May

Border Patrols

A highlight of our rural calendar is the village Open Garden Day, which we heard about with detached interest when we first settled into our cottage. Detached interest turned to panicky shock when we realised that our garden lies at an important strategic position at the foot of the hill leading up to the village. The calm expectation of the Gardening Committee was that we should provide tea and a pretty cottage garden for visitors to rest in before they toiled up the hill to the serious gardens at the top.

The most serious garden of all belongs to Audrey, the terrifyingly knowledgeable doyenne of local gardens and flowers, who also fronts the Gardening Committee. Audrey has been around for so long that she was probably advising on window boxes for the ark ("Please, Noah, no begonias!"). She cornered me in the village shop to ask what had happened to the charming display of tulips our garden had previously shown. "Aly! How deep do you plant your tulips?" "Er, so you can't quite see them?" Wrong answer! "Tulips must be planted ten inches deep so they have to work to break the surface!" My tulips were too obviously layabouts, and I could see that Audrey had me down (with good reason) as a gardening lightweight.

Unlike my predecessors, I spent more time tending our motley crew of animals than I did the garden, and it showed. Flowers popped up in the lawn and grass invaded the borders. I dreamed of the whole lot coming together as one glorious wildflower meadow, but in the real world I weeded and edged and trimmed as Open Garden Day approached at terrifying speed. When it arrived, the garden looked surprised but respectable, and I never wanted to touch a trowel again.

The first visitor's arrival coincided with a massive downpour, which suited me just fine. Nobody was going to notice that the charming feathery plants at the back of my borders were actually cow parsley (how on earth did they get there?) when rain cascaded down their neck. As it turned out the visitors, though soaked, were so appreciative that I began to enjoy myself. I nipped up the hill to see how things were going at the business end of the operation.

Audrey, in full mid-Atlantic trawler gear, was holding court in the centre of the village. Expert on all matters horticultural, she pointed out the garden with Water Features, the garden with Rooms, and the garden with Witty Detail (revolving glass globes above a serpentine pond). The vicar's garden was getting a lot of attention. He has devised a system

of reed beds that process his sewage. The problem is that they are only partially successful. As a neighbour said, "You don't want to be hanging round the vicar's place when the wind's coming from the south-west." Alas, that's where the wind was coming from that day and visitors who went to hear the vicar's impassioned speech on the correct bulrushes/solids balance, tended to leave in a hurry with pale green faces. On the plus side this added to our profits, as they were shepherded straight into the welcoming arms of the small bar facility (courtesy of the Friendly Ferret) where they could settle their stomachs and plan visits to other less challenging gardens.

Mr Addington was in charge of parking, standing sentry against the beastly hordes who tried to park on the verge (free) instead of in the designated field (small charge). His fluorescent tabard gleamed officiously as he flagged down a small car: "Park in the field," he commanded. "But we're on the way to see mum in the next village." "Hah! That's what they all say. You park in the field and pay like everybody else." Audrey, scenting battle like a war horse, swept down the street and swiftly identified and released the occupants of the vehicle.

Later, when we had all dried out and totted up the totals, we found to our joy that Audrey and the garden gang had done it again – the Open Garden Day had been a huge success. Next year I will try harder. I won't let the hens dustbath in the borders, geese snap off flower heads or dogs jump on the perennials. My garden will be a credit to the village – a vision of abundant loveliness at which visitors will gasp. Yeah, right!

Everything's Sheep-Shape

I've always had a problem with shearing. First of all, when to do it? And then, who should do it? Finally, when the shearing is over and your sheep are cool and breezy – what about the fleeces? Pauline, my sheep guru, always gets it right. Her fleeces go off to Wales and return woven into delightful throws, soft blankets and even stylish hats. I collected my fleeces and sent them to a lady in Dorset with a Navajo loom. After a great deal of time (and money) they returned as a rug that looked and smelt like a freshly skinned gorilla. The dogs growled at it, the cat spat at it and the Hoover bag filled up with wool.

So, this year, as the weather warmed, and the sheep panted theatrically when they saw me, my heart sank. Luckily, one is never without advice in the countryside. First up was Colin, a chance meet in the post office. "Haven't you sheared your sheep yet?" he asked, "I saw Ginny yesterday and she did hers three weeks ago!" Ginny has a large and lucrative flock of native breed sheep that supply some famous London restaurants. She is revered locally because no matter how much shepherding she does, her manicure is always immaculate.

I returned to my sheep and dithered. Mr Addington strode by. "Glad to see somebody thinks of the wellbeing of their sheep!" he snapped. "It's appalling how these so-called experts whip their fleeces off early, the next moment it's hailing and then what?" He nodded curtly to me, and went on his way. I was joined by Frank, the village's all-round countryman. "You need to shear those yows," he said sagely. "Bluebottles will spot your lot and then 'zap'!" The hideous spectre of flystrike convinced me. The fleeces must go.

So I progressed to my annual agony over which shearer I should choose. One never-to-be-forgotten year I decided to do my own shearing. I bought a shiny pair of hand shears, read a book about shearing, and lined up Dinky on the barber's stool. It took me a whole hour to shear her and the rest of the day before I could stand upright again. Dinky looked like a bizarre poodle and wouldn't come near me for weeks. No, this was a job for experts. The team of bronzed New Zealanders who sheared Ginny's many sheep at lightning speed wouldn't even consider my flock of five. Anyway, my pampered princesses demanded tact and niceties during the undignified business of being shorn.

Second choice was Harmony Biggins, a hippy with dreadlocks and a psychedelic Morris Traveller, who'd done the shearing since my failed attempt. He's expert with the shears, but likes to live unshackled by manmade constraints so only

shears when he feels like it. His answerphone told me that he had gone to a happening in Nepal. I realised with foreboding that the only option left was the Gribble family.

The Gribbles are a tribe of shepherds who live in a deep, dark Gloucestershire valley and whose forbears didn't get out much for several centuries. They are highly regarded locally as sheep shearers but my problem is that I can't understand a word they say, which is highly embarrassing. But needs must – I dialled their number, and a Gribble answered. "Hurdle wurdle gurdle?" said the voice. I took a deep breath and explained that my sheep needed shearing, and how about next Wednesday? "Wurdle gur. Ar," came the reply. "Great!" I said, weakly, and hoped for the best.

Wednesday dawned fair. My sheep had spent the night indoors, so were dry and very woolly. I hung around hopefully and, oh joy! Bang on time an ancient pick-up arrived, filled to the brim with Gribbles. They were wonderful – gentle with the sheep and cheerful. The language barrier remained, but they were patient with me, and ordered mugs of hot sweet tea in sign language. They left a neat stack of fleeces, and we parted on a tide of mutually incomprehensible goodwill.

Afterwards I watched my happy little flock amble about in the sun looking like velvety pear drops, and felt quietly pleased. This year, I think I got shearing just right.

Natural Selection

Julia, hedge-fund manager and embodiment of the phrase, 'If you want to get something done, ask a busy person', had become a governor of our local primary school. She agreed with its Ofsted rating of 'excellent' in every respect but one – the school had flourishing bird feeders and nest boxes, and a popular vegetable garden, but no nature table to inform or inspire and reflect the passing seasons. So Julia proposed an Eco Morning. Staff, pupils and parents would meet and gather appropriate material from the natural bounty that surrounded and sometimes invaded our homes, from which a vibrant new nature table could be created for the school. Jen, the head teacher, thought this was a great idea and suggested that villagers send in donations, too.

Eco Morning dawned and we gathered at the school for a quick meeting to inspect the offerings that had already arrived. Ralph, our oldest villager and great-grandfather of Angelina (Year 2) had brought in his collection of wild bird eggs, personally assembled in the 1930s. Julia explained tactfully that this would be inappropriate for our eco-friendly nature table so Ralph, unabashed, shuffled home and returned with an ancient two-headed frog preserved in a jar. "The young 'uns always like my frog," he chuckled. Julia swallowed but, anxious not to upset the old man, quietly advised us to dispose of his frog at the earliest opportunity. "We don't want any nightmares," she hissed. The whole school and its supporters headed out to a field suggested as suitable by local farmer Maurice. Here we could seek out nature's goodness, safe in the knowledge that cows hadn't been there first.

Ben, the village joker, was soon showing an enthusiastic group how to make ear splitting shrieks from blowing through a blade of grass. "Thanks for that, Ben!" Jen said. Then Harry, Maurice's son, delightedly produced something he called a minibeast, but I called half a worm. Angelina was holding a multicoloured flower. "That's lovely," Julia said in her best nurturing governor's voice, "where did you discover it?" "At home," Angelina stated, looking at Julia pityingly, "in a vase." But once we started to search properly, the spring countryside positively hurled contributions at us and we returned to school laden with seeds, sheep's wool and eggshells, all ready to be labelled in clear, lower-case script.

On entering the school hall, Julia stopped dead. Ralph's two-headed frog had been unearthed from its hiding place and

placed reverently and centrally on the new nature table. "Please can we lose the frog!" she commanded, but it was too late. Pupils streamed in with their offerings, arranging them with the frog as the focal point. Still, it was time for the workshops, and mine was demonstrating how to blow eggs. I have done this with many a hen's egg for painting at Easter time: you drill a small hole in each end and blow hard in one hole until the contents drain out of the other. I began with a guinea fowl's egg, which was fetchingly speckled but turned out to be harder than granite. I blew vigorously and nothing happened, then harder, and harder still, turning bright purple. Year 2 grouped around me, looking expectant. They had never seen somebody explode before, but were ready for a new experience in the name of scientific enquiry. A bead of yolk appeared at the other end of the egg, and I finally, painfully, blew the thing empty. Breathing deeply I selected a tiny bantam's egg for my next demonstration and blew mightily into it. Big mistake! The fragile shell shattered and egg yolk squirted out at high velocity. This time Year 2's joy was unconfined. They laughed until they fell over, as I wiped a thick layer of yolk from my nose and wearily eyed up the turkey egg that was next. "You see, Year 2", said their teacher, "nature study is sometimes messy and always surprising!"

The fun over, we returned to the hall, where Angelina was proudly displaying her great-grandfather's freakish frog to a crowd of admirers. Pupils from all classes were arriving to marvel at the treasure. For the future, Jen and Julia had great plans for pond dipping and a nest-box web cam. But today, they had to stand back and let Ralph's frog take centre stage as the undoubted star of the school's new nature table.

Magic Moments

It was one of those late spring days when lambing is over, the weather is warming up and the garden isn't yet overwhelmed by weeds. I wandered out of the cottage and headed towards the sheep field with a song in my heart and a bunch of ivy (my sheep love it) in my hand. Ahead I could see the easily recognisable figure of Mr Addington. I didn't rush to catch up, as his conversation usually has more in common with bleak January than glad May, but then I noticed something unusual.

Mr Addington hadn't spotted me and was going out of his way to splash in every puddle that a recent shower had liberally provided in the lane. He was wearing a pair of gleaming Wellington boots that looked as if they were on their first outing and which left a satisfying trail of silvery wet footprints. I found the sight surprisingly heart-warming: Mr Addington, not an easy man, was revelling in a private moment of happiness – two moments, if you count his obvious pleasure in owning shiny new wellies

Presently, I was joined by my neighbour Frank and his new wife Phyllis. Frank was wielding a hazel twig and vigorously indulging in his favourite spring pastime – whacking the heads off the massed ranks of cow parsley that throng our lanes. It's a controversial pleasure, and when I first arrived here I asked him why he was so brutal to a delightful and harmless flower. After deep thought he replied: "I can't stand the b*****s," and there the matter rested. The cow parsley certainly fights back but at this time of year you can track where Frank has been walking by a trail of mangled blooms.

Phyllis has her own particular pleasure; a keen experimental cook, she loves collecting wild foods as her raw materials. She entertains generously, but regular guests know to remain alert and carry a packet of indigestion tablets. You should be safe with her unidentified Meat Pie and her Hedgerow Crumble, but her Dried Fungi Surprise recently put Frank in hospital. This was not ideal, though good news for the cow parsley. "I was doing all right until Phyllis brought me some of her berry muffins," he told me. "That put me back a bit, but I'm better now." I congratulated him on his return to health and at the same time surreptitiously checked that the blooms Phyllis was gathering into her wicker basket were nothing more toxic than early elderflowers.

A loud yapping proclaimed the arrival of the local gardening queen. Audrey gardens ferociously and also collects terriers, five of which were revolving in a scrabbling maypole around her as she marched down the lane. "Wonderful day for a dog walk!" Audrey trumpeted, oblivious to the terriers' five extendable leads, which were forming a complicated cats' cradle around our legs. We disentangled and she strode away, to be replaced by Colin, going for a power walk.

For reasons of his own, Colin dresses in Lycra cycling shorts and carries two walking poles to walk, but he never strays far from the village. "Good morning!" he boomed. "I've discovered a marvellous new view. Have you got time to come and see it?" I didn't really have time, but I trudged in Colin's wake hoping to see an as yet undiscovered Iron

Age fort or crop circle. Colin halted at the summit. "Look!" he cried. "If you stand here you can see the M4 through those two trees!" I briefly entertained a futile thought that he was joking. But no, he gazed entranced at the distant glittering ribbon of traffic, while I enjoyed all the other bits of landscape that didn't contain a busy motorway.

I retraced my steps back down to the field and gave some ivy leaves to Teazle, my favourite sheep. Her topaz eyes half closed in sheer bliss and I reflected on the satisfaction gained from chatting to a friendly animal. In fact, the whole morning had showed the ways in which my neighbours enjoy their daily round, those little things that make our rural life a constant delight despite the niggles of icy roads in winter, the funereal speed of local broadband and just about everything to do with mud. Whether it is harvesting wild food, walking dogs, sploshing in puddles or motorway spotting, these simple pleasures significantly increase the sum of human happiness in our village.

Phyllis' hedgerow secrets

Well I love to go out and about in our local copses and dingles, searching for nature's bounty. In many a hidden byway I've discovered an unexpected prize to take home and turn into a culinary treat for my husband Frank. You've got to be careful with mushrooms, mind. I put Frank in hospital last year with my Dried Fungi Surprise. But I've been on a course now and I'm fairly confident it won't happen again. I take my lidded wicker basket and I fill it with what I glean. Seeds, berries, snails – if it's nutritious it goes into my basket. In May it'll be flowers and herbs, and of course roadkill is in season whatever the time of year.

Here are some of my springtime favourites. I've tested them out on Frank and he seems fine so far:

Nettle soup
1 nice big onion, chopped
3 cloves garlic, chopped
Half a carrier bag of young nettle tips (pick these with gloves on!)
2 medium potatoes, diced
1 litre stock
Salt, pepper and nutmeg
2 tablespoons cream

Sauté onion and garlic in a large saucepan. Pour scalding water on nettles (this takes the sting out of them). Chop and add them to onions and garlic. Add potatoes, cover with stock and simmer until tender. Season with salt, pepper and nutmeg and add cream to serve.

Elderflower cordial
50g citric acid
2 small lemons, quartered
1.2kg granulated sugar
1.5 litre boiling water
Large bunch elderflower heads

Put elderflowers, citric acid, lemons and sugar into boiling water, remove from heat and steep for 48 hours. Filter through muslin into sterilised bottles. Will keep for 8 weeks in fridge. Dilute with sparkling spring water to serve.

It's a pity there's not quite room for my Roadkill Ratatouille. Now there's a recipe with a bit of body to it!

June

Game, Set and Match

When Colin first arrived in our village, fresh from London, he was determined to live the rural life. He would grow roses, keep bees and play tennis. But things didn't all go quite as planned. He blasted his carefully planted roses with a chemical arsenal but still they suffered from blight and the bees fled his property in a buzzing swarm. However, the tennis flourished and Colin's tournament became an important fixture on the village calendar, with Colin outshining most of us as a player. Year after year his name was engraved on the silver Singles Cup and yet the thrill of winning never wore thin.

Colin's campaign began early, and he nobbled churchgoers as they filed past the vicar on Easter Sunday. "You'll come to my tennis tournament? Last week in June? Splendid!" Colin trod on the vicar's toe in his enthusiasm. "Sorry vicar, you'll be coming along to watch? We'll find you a nice shady place to sit down in." The vicar looked thoughtfully at Colin, while he rubbed his foot. "Do you know, I'm usually busy in June but this year I really think I'll enter." Colin looked startled. "Well, you can always pull out if it's too much for you." And there the matter rested until the day itself.

Colin welcomed us into his garden, jaunty in sparkling whites with a striped tie fastened around his waist in place of a belt. Mr Addington sat importantly on a stepladder from where he could intone "love – 15" with a wonderfully Wimbledon-like delivery, and some handsomely paid village children stood by as ballboys. The stage was set for another of Colin's triumphs. The vicar arrived, wearing white trousers, a long-sleeved white shirt and the floppy linen hat he wore for gardening. Colin watched in horror as he methodically began to undo his ancient wooden tennis racket from its equally ancient wooden press. "Oh dear, vicar, do you really think you are up to this?" "Yes," said the vicar equably. "I really think I am." Colin shrugged his shoulders, glanced admiringly down at his own racket, a modern marvel of carbon fibre, and bounced off on hosting duties.

Most of us locals were mediocre players. Occasional good shots, accompanied by a gasp of astonishment from the player, were balanced by really bad shots right out of court or straight into the bottom of the net. One by one we left the court, vanquished, to mutual commiseration and a glass of consoling Pimm's. And this is when we realised that our vicar, his thick glasses sparkling in the sun, had been calmly winning every game. In fact he was going to play Colin in the finals.

Colin was now wearing his striped tie around his head in the manner of a Japanese kamikaze fighter pilot. He raced wildly about, grunting when he hit the ball and sweating profusely. But the vicar, who appeared to stroll around the court, was always in the right place and drew inexorably ahead. When they paused for refreshment between games, Colin sat by the net and called for towels and water bottles. But the vicar went for a potter around the outside of the court, gazing interestedly at Colin's climbing roses, which dripped with mildew and aphids.

The vicar duly won the match, and I stood next to his wife Joan as the Singles Cup was presented. "Your husband was amazing!" I said to her. "Yes," replied Joan serenely, "he played in Junior Wimbledon before he went to theology college. It's nice for him to have an occasional game. He so seldom has the leisure." It was the vicar's day, game, set and match. And on his way out, he pressed a jar of honey from his busy vicarage bees into Colin's hands.

Yet Colin remained buoyant. "No shame in losing to a Wimbledon player!" he remarked later. "Marvellous chap, the vicar. He's started me on a pruning and mulching programme for my roses that he promises will sort them out." Colin may have been beaten at tennis, but he felt he had taken one important step closer to the rural idyll he had dreamed of. Who wouldn't be happy about that?

What's in a Name?

Jigsaw, my coloured cob, is a girl of many moods. When we decide to hack through the village, she sometimes chooses to blast down the streets like a tank trying for the land speed record. On other days she may be in go-slow mode, and riding a circuit of the village has much in common with pushing a JCB uphill. With the handbrake on. These are the days when I have leisure to study the names of village houses as we amble gently past them.

House numbers haven't made it to our corner of Wiltshire yet. It's left to our imagination and ingenuity to label our homes to guide the relief postman (our regular postman doesn't need any more than his well-worn internal map flagged up with the various dogs and cups of tea he expects as he works his way around the parish). As Jigsaw and I enter the village, several house names speak of a departed golden age

– The Old Laundry, The Old Dairy, The Old School House. Our descendants may one day name their houses with similar nostalgia – The Old Internet Café, The Old Diversified Farm.

Some names are straightforward: The Thatched Cottage, The White House. This call-a-spade-a-spade school of house naming has Frank as our neighbourhood champion. Frank, after an intensely fought round of local and planning politics, found himself the delighted owner of a brand new house in the village centre. It needed a name, and after weeks of impassioned debate and reviewing of options in the village shop, he chose it: The Bungalow. Which has the single merit of being factually spot-on.

On the other hand some house names contain an element of mystery, or wishful thinking. As we meander past a pretty house called Sweet Winds, Jigsaw's long nose wrinkles in disgust – the name would ring a truer note if the house was situated slightly further from Maurice's slurry pit. Some of the older houses bear witness to an earlier and more robust use of names. Bottom Cottage was built in a bottom, or valley as some call it. It bore its name proudly for many years and then it was bought by Colin. In very short order, a large extension and a conservatory were added and Bottom Cottage metamorphosised into Fieldview House. Colin is an important man. He drives an important car, and says important things. But some local memories have stamina. Colin would be distraught to know it, but he is universally referred to as 'that Colin from the Bottom'.

On the far side of the village we pass a square stone house in immaculate gardens. When Mr Addington bought it, he was delighted with its name: Bustard House. 'Bustards!" he thought. 'Magnificent birds. Splendid!' That was before he met Ben. Ben is the village's human equivalent of a Labrador – brimming over with boundless and sometimes inappropriate bouncy good humour. Ben was inspired to drag Mr and Mrs

Addington up to the vicar at the church Pancake Supper and say: "Vicar! Meet Mr and Mrs Addington, a right pair of Bustards! Heh! Heh! Heh!" A brisk phone call and some hasty paperwork later, and Bustard House became The Laurels, a title guaranteed to draw a line under any amusing name-calling.

By now, Jigsaw and I were reaching the home straight – a lane known as Edgecorner Lake. But there is no reed encircled, moor-hen haunted stretch of water here, just a dusty little road. Some years ago, Frank was minding his own business in Hedgecorner Lane when he was approached by a council official with a clipboard, who asked him the name of the road they were standing on. Frank is a courteous countryman, but he doesn't do strangers, so he muttered something along the lines of "'edgecorner, like" and beat a hasty retreat. Some weeks later a shiny new road sign announced to a startled village that the lane was called Edgecorner Lake, and the new name has now stuck fast.

Jigsaw quickened her pace, intent on a spot of pampering followed by speed-eating in her field, and our stone cottage appeared around the corner. And what is its name? After our little circuit, Dun Rubbernecking would seem about right. At least for this month.

By Hook or by Crook

Every year at midsummer we host a croquet tournament. By tradition the weather is glorious, our garden looks as good as it can do with its multiple handicaps of geese, hens and the odd escaped sheep, and the villagers are in party mode. Our lawn has some natural hazards, which include a few molehills and Tallulah the tortoise, but these are well known and negotiable by most. So why did I always feel a growing sense of apprehension as match day approached?

The reason, as I remembered each time the competition was in full swing, is that croquet can bring out the very worst in people. I know my neighbours well and would have trusted most of them with my life, even Ben who is reliably unreliable. But give them a mallet and a croquet ball and they turn into cheating con men (and women – the unsporting antics that go on are entirely equal opportunities), each prepared to pawn their granny in order to secure victory and the chocolate Champagne bottle that accompanies it.

Then the guests arrived, the Pimm's started flowing, the first game got under way and I forgot my fears and started to enjoy the occasion. The villagers entered into the spirit of the game and wore Panama hats, striped blazers and summer dresses. I acted as umpire, guiding the players around the course and filling in results on the leader board, a sheet of A3 paper pinned to the garden shed. It was going well and the party was convivial and fun with a competitive edge. Our lawn is bounded on one side by a steep bank that leads down to rough grass and is the croquet equivalent of a golfing bunker. Known locally as the 'Slope of Despair' (SoD), the players kept well away from it at first. That is, until the last round…

The four finalists were Colin, who has an overdeveloped competitive streak, Ben, the prankster, fastidious Mr Addington and Anna. I was keeping a watchful eye on Ben when I heard Mrs Addington say disapprovingly to her husband: "Wallace! I saw that!" When I swung around to investigate, Mr Addington was standing innocently by his ball and Mrs Addington clearly wasn't going to elaborate. Meanwhile, Colin had knocked Ben's ball straight down the SoD. As though trained to it, Ben's black Labrador Bodger immediately invaded the pitch, seized Colin's croquet ball and galloped off with it. As I chased after Bodger and retrieved Colin's ball, Ben rejoined the game and vied with Mr Addington for the lead.

It was at this tense moment that Tallulah the tortoise woke up from her snooze in the shrubbery and decided on a slow-motion sprint across the croquet lawn. Animal lover Mr Addington paused to watch her but not so Colin, who seized upon his lapse in concentration and knocked the Addington ball down the SoD. But his evil plan was foiled by Tallulah when she stopped in front of the hoop he was about to tap his ball through, pulled her legs in and went back to sleep. Colin dithered and Ben knocked Colin's ball down the now crowded SoD. He then woke Tallulah up, tempted her away from the hoop with a dandelion and before anyone could object, tapped his ball against the striped pole in the middle of the lawn to make him the winner.

As we presented him with his chocolate Champagne bottle to the cheers of the crowd, who had largely ignored the antics on the pitch, Mr Addington and Colin were still at the bottom of the SoD, locked in a circular argument over whose fault it was that they had both lost. Anna came up to me quietly. "I didn't like to make a fuss," she said, "but Ben missed out the final hoop!" I looked over to where the victor was shamelessly lapping up congratulations and I gave Anna a consoling glass of Pimm's. And took one for myself.

I'm sure that by next year I will have forgotten the rampant gamesmanship and will just remember the laughter and the Panama hats. But maybe it is somebody else's turn to be umpire.

Wedding Belle

When William announced his engagement, the village was startled (to put it mildly). William was a tall, quiet chap with a passionate interest in Land Rovers. He had a collection of them, in various stages of repair, which he kept in a neat line in his parents' driveway. When he wasn't working at a nearby garage, he was tinkering with his beloved cars. His schedule left no time for dalliance, nor did William seem to desire any such thing. It had been accepted for a long time that, if it didn't have chunky wheels and a safari snorkel, William just wasn't interested.

And now he was engaged, and the wedding date was set. I encountered William's mother in the village shop. She is a stylish lady, well into her seventh decade, and she was discussing wedding clothes with Anna, our postmistress. "I'm not having a hat," she said decisively. "I'm going to wear one of those fornicators. You know, just a little bunch of feathers and such." Anna and I exchanged carefully expressionless glances. "I think you'd look lovely in a fascinator," Anna said, with great emphasis. I agreed, tremulously.

I met William's fiancée in our local, The Friendly Ferret, that night and could see that this had the potential to be a perfect partnership. Cherry had flowing fair hair, was built on Amazonian lines, and had an air of mechanical competence. You knew immediately when you met Cherry that here was a girl who could handle a torque wrench.

With the wedding fast approaching, the village swung into action. We get quite a few funerals here but not that many weddings, and the community prepared to party. Audrey took over the wedding flowers. I wasn't allowed anywhere near advanced matters such as the bride's bouquet, but I was permitted to do some of the little displays to hang on the ends of every pew. Mr Addington seized the chance to be officious in a fluorescent tabard and offered to take charge of parking arrangements. A local band was engaged to play at the reception. They had started life as strolling medieval players and, after a brief flirtation with barn dances, had found their true vocation playing covers of 80s hits at local gatherings.

Although it was high summer, it was raining heavily on the wedding day. So instead of arriving on Maurice's rose festooned farm trailer, as had been planned, the bride and bridesmaids journeyed to church in William's favourite Land Rover. This was prepared for the honeymoon (driving overland to Turkey) and was loaded with jerry cans and strapped-down boxes, on which the wedding party had to squat. Nothing daunted, Cherry clambered out at the church and looked radiant as she walked down the aisle. I had expected her wedding dress to be classical and severe, cut to show off her biceps, but not a bit of it. She was triumphant in a froth of feminine frills.

William himself was a bit damp around the edges as he had driven over in the Land Rover that currently had the roof removed, but they said their vows with enthusiasm and made a truly striking couple. The sun came out for long enough to bless the bride with a few watery rays for photographs and then the rain set in heavily for the afternoon. I wasn't the only one to accessorise my wedding outfit with a pair of floral wellies, as we splashed our way to the village hall.

In keeping with tradition, the wedding presents were displayed on a long table. Among the more customary gifts of towel sets and saucepans were some less conventional items such as a sledgehammer and a folding spade. William's friends knew their man. The wedding reception was a delight and the mother of the groom danced elegantly to a Wham! hit, her fascinator bobbing proudly in her silver hair.

As the happy couple's Land Rover growled throatily off into the darkness trailing numerous rattling oil cans behind it, Cherry's brawny arm waved the folding spade cheerfully at us from the passenger window. Those of us left behind in the driving rain were all in complete agreement: this, surely, was a match made in heaven.

Cherry's collected ideas for a country wedding

We had a beautiful wedding, we really did! It was a special day th
will stay in our hearts forever. And what really touched us was
the way the villagers rallied round to support us with all sorts
of suggestions. We couldn't have done it without them, and here ar
some of their very best ideas:

Wedding cake. Noreen's a wonderful cook, and she made us a towe
of cupcakes instead of a fruitcake. Because she knows William, she
iced the cupcakes in Land Rover colours.

Confetti. Paper confetti isn't allowed so Anna told everybody ho
to make confetti out of real rose petals. You either spread them on
tissue paper in the airing cupboard and leave them for a couple
of days, or you place them on kitchen roll and microwave for one
minute on either side. The vicar was delighted!

Bunting. I'm all thumbs when it comes to sewing, so Joan showed
me a simple way to make bunting. You gather together fabric, bias
binding tape and pinking shears. You draw a triangle on cardboard
use it as a template on the fabric, and cut out the fl ag shapes
with pinking shears. Then you pin the fl ags along your bias
binding and sew them on with a straight run on a sewing machine.

Table arrangements. Audrey came up with this one. I went round
the charity shops and bought some cream jugs, then Audrey arrange
a little posy in each one for table centrepieces.

Place names. This idea was all my own. I found a lovely spanner
set at a car boot sale and painted our guests' names on each
spanner in pink and cream. They matched the roses something
lovely. And the guests took the spanners home as wedding favours.

July

Dancing Queen

Mrs Addington's spectacles glittered as she surveyed the people she termed 'key players of the village' but who could equally well be called 'mugs who didn't run fast enough' that she'd gathered together in her house. "I've had a splendid idea," she said. "We'll hold a barn dance!" She painted a delightful picture of the village skipping in a simple and wholesome way to time-honoured tunes, then bonding over a nutritionally balanced meal. Seeing our dubious expressions, Mrs Addington's jaw jutted resolutely. "It will be splendid," she repeated, "and I shall organise it!" We cheered up slightly. Bright ideas on village bonding were all very well, but somebody had to see them through.

When we met again, Mrs Addington had got onto the case. She confirmed that Maurice would lend his barn, told us that some friends would provide music and caller, and said that if we insisted on puddings (we did) we should bring fruit salad. Then she looked at her watch, exclaimed "Meetings, meetings! I'm afraid that I need your space," and shooed us out of her house. It took the rest of us 30 seconds to decide on the nutritionally balanced meal: fish (protein) and chips (carbohydrate), which we could pre-order from the chip van, and everyone would bring their favourite pudding.

On Barn Dance Day we met early to set up the barn. The trestle table was already covered with puddings, and it was obvious that in the village's eyes the main food groups were cream, chocolate, sugar and jam. Not a fruit salad in sight.

We waited for Mrs Addington to appear but she didn't come. The musicians arrived, and started lovingly unwrapping their instruments, which were not the fiddle, guitar and drum kit we had been expecting. I went up to a man with a straggling grey beard. "Do you do many barn dances?" I asked, casually. He smiled shyly: "No, we're strolling medieval players, but we've decided to diversify. This is our first barn dance." He proudly pointed out a man holding a book entitled Idiot's Guide to Barn Dance Calling. "Harry usually does mumming, but today he's our caller." "Ah." I walked thoughtfully back to our little group of 'key players' and told them the news: our inaugural barn dance was going to be danced to the accompaniment of a lute, sackbut and portable set of virginals.

The villagers arrived in gratifying numbers. Some wore cowboy gear, under the impression it was a themed Western evening. Some were straight off the tractor, while others wore suits and cocktail dresses. But it was not until the fish and chips

were a greasy memory that Mrs Addington finally arrived and sank down on a chair with a groan. She had a migraine and wasn't going to organise anything.

The band struck up a medieval tune and Harry the caller bashfully began: "Take your partners, and…no, everybody link hands, and…oh sorry, I missed a page…" Lacking clear direction, we became a disorderly rabble. Punters started leaving the dancing, heading purposefully to the puddings or drifting towards the doors.

At this point Julia entered, straight off the train from London and still in her hedge fund manager's uniform of sharp suit and big pearls. She gazed disbelievingly at the die-hards attempting to dance the Gay Gordons to the tune of Greensleeves while Harry bleated miserably from behind his book. Julia marched over to the band and told them to play something lively, removed us from the pudding table and exits by sheer force of personality, and got going. Harry sloped off, relieved, into the shadows. Some minutes later Mrs Addington opened a bleary eye. Julia was energetically screaming the village through Strip the Willow to the tune of Sumer is Icumen In and everyone was dancing, whirling, shouting 'cuckoo!' and generally having the time of their lives. In her weakened state of tunnel vision and flashing lights, Mrs A couldn't do a thing about it, but this clearly wasn't what she had in mind at all.

And yet we had a great evening. After the dancing, when the medieval players had been fondly waved off, we finished the puddings down to the last smear of cream. We bonded spectacularly, and still shout 'cuckoo!' when we meet on the street. The Village Barn Dance may well become an annual affair. So though Mrs Addington's lips tighten noticeably whenever the event is mentioned, it really was splendid.

Supper is Served

Since arriving in our village, I have learned many things. One is that you would be lost without a good pair of wellies. Another is that a convivial gathering of neighbours, in a house close enough to walk to, can offer the very finest entertainment. Also that villagers tend to have a soft, verging on blind, spot about their pets. All of these discoveries were recently brought into sharp focus when Pammy, who lives at the other end of the village, invited me to supper.

The evening was warm, but I carried my shoes and wore wellies to walk to her cottage. So did the other guests, because nobody wants to arrive having just stepped in something unfortunate. A beautifully laid table awaited us in her garden, a vision of polished silver, crystal and china. The jarring note was the ominous purple thunder cloud suspended over her garden. Colin, a neighbour, looked up as our hostess offered a welcoming drink: "Lovely, Pammy, but it's going to rain." "No, the weatherman said not until tomorrow!" she retorted. Fat raindrops began to fall. "But they promised!" Pammy wailed, as we formed a human chain and rushed the finery back into the cottage.

As we sat down in Pammy's little dining room, a huge cat jumped onto my lap. Pammy is a businesswoman who handles a large workforce with tact and firmness, but it was obvious she was putty in this cat's paws. "That's Muffles," she said proudly. "He'll be fine as long as you don't move." Muffles looked at me with a cold, green stare and unsheathed all his claws. I took the hint, and decided to stay put.

We were well into the soup course, with Muffles acting as combined hot water bottle and table napkin, and I was chatting to Matt, Julia's husband, when a stream of water from above hit him on the head. "The gutter! It's blocked!

Quick!" shrieked Pammy. The assembled company jumped up and clattered up the stairs. I couldn't follow because Muffles didn't shift, and I was pinned to my chair. After some bumping noises from upstairs, the waterfall lessened and then stopped. Colin led the procession back into the dining room, soaked but triumphant and I was told the stirring tale of how the vicar had helped Colin out of an upstairs window to clear the gutter in the thatch.

Excitement over, Pammy rushed into the kitchen to collect the main course and Muffles jumped down to my intense relief and followed her out to supervise. I then heard a loud 'splat' followed by a hysterical giggle from Pammy. Hurrying to investigate, I opened the kitchen door to see a mound of fragrantly steaming garlic chicken on the floor, with Muffles growling possessively over a morsel he had hooked from the

wreckage. "I tripped over Muffles," Pammy explained. "Aly, do you think…?" Yes, I did think. Our supper had fallen on a gleamingly clean floor and anyway, I was so hungry I didn't care. We shovelled the chicken back onto its plate and served it up. And it tasted lovely, despite its adventures.

It was later, as we were enjoying an excellent cheesecake, that Muffles re-entered and stuck an exploratory claw into Julia's leg from under the table. Julia screamed and spilt her glass of red wine on the cloth. Colin, now a self-styled man of action, unhesitatingly tipped his glass of white wine on top of the red. "That'll stop it staining," he said. The vicar gazed at the pool of newly blended rosé spreading rapidly on the snowy damask. "That would indeed be a miracle," he said thoughtfully.

Coffee was served in the sitting room, where Muffles stretched himself out on the carpet and slashed at passing ankles. Pammy bravely scooped him up. "He's just a big softie, really," she assured us, despite plentiful evidence to the contrary. We waved goodbye to Pammy and Muffles, who was stropping his claws on the Jane Churchill curtains, and set off to walk to our various homes through a lane deep in puddles. As we went, we agreed that it had been a lovely evening - friendly company, delicious food and (so important) never a dull moment!

Supporting Roles

One of the many joys of joining a village community is discovering over the years the infinite variety of its inhabitants. Who would guess at first acquaintance, for example, that Rachael the churchwarden is a nationally respected judge of fancy rats? Or that gentle William, the proprietor of the local garage, is an enthusiastic member of a historical re-enactment group who can be seen at weekends stuffing his pike into his Land Rover and trundling off to war? Or that Maurice the farmer is a fanatical amateur thespian, and won a rose bowl for acting in his salad days? Ben, an extrovert, has found his natural home in a team of morris dancers, and my neighbour Frank has spent years perfecting a method of making combustible fuel – out of sheep droppings.

Our village is supportive by nature. In the same way that we give an elderly neighbour a lift to the doctor's surgery, or all turn out to search for Kay's kunekune pig when she bulldozes through the fence and vanishes yet again, we wouldn't dream of letting Maurice emote to an empty theatre. His farming duties only allow him time to learn his lines once a year, but when the moment comes that he enters, stage right, he can count upon an audience of enthusiastic supporters. His wife rewards our faithfulness by handing round luscious plates of eats when the

play is over. But delightful though it is to revive ourselves with ham sandwiches as Maurice, flushed and radiant, accepts our plaudits, we would come even without the food. Just because Maurice is a villager.

Rachael's judging duties tend to take her to far-flung village halls but some of us have followed her to act as steward, and admire her calm authority as she strolls in her white coat between the rustling ranks of show rats. No doubt some of the villagers wrestle with the enhanced status of an animal they see as trouble, but still the village is proud of her - rats and all.

It's easier to show loyalty to William's hobby. When his group performed a re-enactment of a local Civil War battle, practically all his neighbours attended in a convoy of four-wheel drives. Parking near the crest of a hill, we watched with bemusement as our placid William charged red-faced and yelling at an army of Roundheads, who were soon in full retreat.

The vicar turned to Maurice as the whole battle swept over a far swell of the downs with William running strongly in the vanguard. "Didn't the Roundheads win this battle?" he asked. "Not today, I think," replied Maurice.

We don't have to go anywhere to encourage Ben, as every July his morris dancing team spends a happy afternoon performing at the Friendly Ferret and downing vast quantities of Old Ferret ale. We all relish the spectacle of a team of grown men dressed in bells and flowery hats leaping friskily about in astonishingly intricate dances. Publican Ed appreciates the feel-good atmosphere the dancers bring with them as well as the truly astounding bar takings; and the dancers themselves enjoy the warm welcome and the certainty of finding a volunteer to hold an umbrella over the accordion should we be blessed with a summer shower. Ben joins in energetically, and except for the dreadful year when he couldn't resist hitting Mr Addington on the back of the head with a bladder on a stick, the whole event is hugely enjoyable. Even then the day was saved when Mrs Addington, a fervent supporter of all things traditional, decided (quite wrongly) that Ben's actions were symbolic. And once we had recovered his bifocals from where they had been knocked, Mr Addington was in agreement and bought the whole team another pint of Old Ferret, which they celebrated in a crescendo of jingling bells and waving handkerchiefs.

As for Frank and his rural recycling work, I doubt that we will be stoking our woodburning stoves with his output. Although he has patented the name – 'Ewe-ll Logs' – the product is not yet user-friendly and is characterised by its oily black smoke and decidedly less-than fragrant aroma. Supportive though the community is, there are limits!

The Pet Set

A stranger entering our village and strolling along its single street could be forgiven for thinking that our local pet keeping habits are entirely predictable. A Labrador might be seen, trotting companionably alongside its owner, or a terrier might pause from hole-digging on the lawn to greet them at a garden gate. A cat might be spotted going about its private business (our village is well blessed with cats thanks to the commendable work ethic of tabby Kipper, the pub Tom) and it could all seem a bit of a cliché.

However if this visitor were to look more closely, a very different picture would unfold. Mr and Mrs Addington, for example, are devoted to their slinky Siamese cat Ming and her surprisingly large and stripy sons (another notch for Kipper), and the cats reward this love by draping themselves attractively over the sun loungers. But then there are Mrs Addington's hens. She gives a nurturing home to shell-shocked ex-battery fowl, and her latest batch recently arrived completely naked. A three-line whip went out to the Knitting Club and we were summoned to an emergency summit. Mrs Addington, skilled in so many ways, is cack-handed at knitting and needed immediate assistance, so we all created chicken jumpers in double-quick time. Joan, the vicar's wife and a beautiful knitter, put a Fair Isle yoke on her hen jersey, while Julia the hedge-fund manager (not to be outdone) worked hers in a cashmere blend. I created my own chicken cardi in green and red stripes, which looked quite fetching until the hen in question started to sprout bright orange feathers. As the rainbow flock gathers round Mrs Addington while she feeds them lovingly with organic tonics, they all look like pets to me.

Then there is my next-door neighbour Kay's kunekune pig Frimble. Kay's fences are as full of holes as a crocheted doily, and Frimble makes full use of this to escape and patrol the village. Her genial personality makes her popular wherever she roams, and she often finishes up with a pint at the Friendly Ferret where she has a reputation as a bon viveur.

Back home in our stone cottage, the distinction between indoor pet and outside domestic animal is hopelessly blurred. As well as our dogs and another of the Addington kittens, we have an indoor rabbit, while outside my favourite sheep Teazle will shake hands to order and would certainly consider herself to be a pet. Several of the sporadically laying bantams will happily sit on my shoulder in the manner of a pirate's parrot.

But the pet that steals the show is Nigel, our peacock. Nigel came into our lives as a large white egg, furtively presented by an anonymous donor (Frank, himself an obsessive collector of ferrets in private life). I thought it was a goose egg, and placed it in our little incubator with some others. So when the moment of hatching arrived, I was more than a little surprised to find a large white chick with a punk hairstyle and huge,

intelligent eyes struggling out of its egg alongside all the little rubber-billed goslings. Frank was not forthcoming about the peachick's origins, but he took a paternal interest in his progress. Nigel's outsized personality made itself felt from the start, when he struggled out of the box containing his little fuzzy friends, headed straight to the Aga and adopted it as his own personal space. He grew rapidly in size and beauty, and when he was finally evicted from the kitchen (to the dogs' relief), he purloined an apple tree in the garden as his centre of operations – somewhere to grab a bite to eat and snatch forty winks.

Nigel approves of barbecues, where he alternately displays at our guests and snatches any morsel that falls to the ground. He hates indoor supper parties and stands on the windowsill, tapping at the pane and honking disapprovingly at being excluded. He loves Land Rovers because he can stand on their chunky wings to admire his beautiful self in the windscreen. He despises sports cars, whose aerodynamic lines don't give sufficient purchase to his scrabbling claws. Funnily enough, sports car owners don't go a bundle on Nigel, either. Rather to our relief, he hasn't yet discovered love and reserves all his passion for our hedgehog-shaped boot scraper. Frank called round the other day and watched Nigel displaying to the prickles, quivering his tail with little squeaks of excitement. "Give the lad time," he said, rather doubtfully.

So my advice to a visitor would be to look beyond the Labradors: Nigel is living proof that when it comes to our village's pets, it is best not to have pre-conceived notions!

Franks ferreting tips

Ferrets are twisty little beggars, they're as slick as eels. Lovely little thi
mind you. I'd rather watch Jill and Hob running races up my sitting room
curtains than watch TV and that's the truth. I've kept ferrets for I do
know how many years, and I've got some tips to pass on:

Keep them smelling acceptable: ferrets can pong something chronic, makes
even my eyes water sometimes. Phyllis says that if they get up into your sm
drawer just the once, you've got to throw the whole lot away and start ag
If you have them neutered they don't whiff hardly at all. Train them to a
litter box and clean it out every day and you're sorted.

Keep them happy: take them out of their cage every day and let them ru
around in a safe place. Give them tough toys and a cardboard box with hol
cut in. Ferrets are always on the go, except when they're asleep.

Keep them well fed: what ferrets really want is fresh rabbit. But if you
don't fancy preparing raw meat, you can buy dry ferret food that suits the
a treat.

Keep them cosy: ferrets need a warm, dark bedroom with a soft nest in it.
Best thing for their nest is an old fleece or sweatshirt.

Keep them safe: ferrets are built slinky-long and curious, and they can get
through tiny holes. So think like a ferret and check that they can't escape,
because once they get outdoors you'll be lucky to see them again. Houdini isn
in it when you come to ferrets.

And finally:

Keep the sticking plaster handy: and perhaps some iodine. Mine used to nip
a bit but it's only play, most of the time. Some don't nip at all. Be gentle
but firm if they do and say 'No!' Usually works except when they're startled
and that's when you'll need the sticking plaster.

August

Horsing Around

I was sitting in Rachael's kitchen, playing with her baby and trying to stop her terrier Trevor from using my ankle to compensate for the absence of available tottie. Trevor's dodgy social life was the bane of local bitch-owners, though the bitches themselves thought he was great. Rachael passed me the schedule of the local horse show. "You should take Jigsaw," she said. I wasn't convinced. Jigsaw is a fine figure of a horse – you can feel the cottage shake when she does a fly-past in her field – but she has her little ways. There was also myself to consider. In my extreme youth every summer weekend involved loading my adored pony Tiffin into a scruffy old trailer and going out to do battle in the potato race, but those days were long past. "There's a class for coloured horses," Rachael added temptingly. 'Coloured' covers many of the two-toned shades and if there's one thing Jigsaw does really well, it's being black-and-white. When scrubbed up she's as glossy as a magpie, with plenty of stage presence. Perhaps she deserved a wider audience… I sent in my entry.

On show day I arrived early to let Jigsaw soak up some of the atmosphere before she hit centre stage. Several local characters were helping out in various ways: Colin, rigid with importance, was stewarding in the main ring. As the judge selected a horse, Colin would approach it with bowler hat raised and usher it to the centre of the ring with the same formality used by Black Rod to summon MPs to the House of Lords. The village postmistress Anna was in the Secretary's tent, handing out numbers with a reassuring smile that cheered even the most nervous of competitors. Mr Addington was having the time of his life being officious with a two-way radio and special tabard in the parking lines, and Frank was setting up the terrier racing in a small but vocal ring at the edge of the showground.

Jigsaw and I approached the collecting ring to weigh up the opposition. This came in all shapes and sizes, mostly exuding professionalism and a triumph of the equine hairdresser's art. Jigsaw has an amazing ability to grow hair, which I trim to prevent her looking like Dougal from The Magic Roundabout. I could now see that in the showing world this was a mistake – other similar horses had been encouraged to be as hirsute as possible.

We entered the ring and the next few minutes were a blur as I tried to disguise Jigsaw's natural exuberance while we bounded around in a circle at a variety of speeds. After a while, I noticed Colin staring at me with his bowler hat in the air. He had obviously held this position for several minutes, and his smile was becoming frozen. "Do go into the middle, Aly," he said through gritted teeth. We were at the wrong end of the front row, and I had plenty of leisure to admire the main contenders as they were stripped of their saddles and trotted in front of the judge. When our turn came I led Jigsaw out for her moment on the catwalk, and managed to thwart her plans as she measured up the judge for a swift kick as she strode past him. She did her best, but I could see that to head the line she would have needed hair extensions all round and a total change of attitude. Then it was saddles back on and round for another lap before Colin called us in again for our final placings.

Back in Tiffin's day, rosettes went to fourth place. If the class was particularly huge an extra pink rosette might be added with 'Special' written across it to show that, although you were hopeless, you were not quite as hopeless as all the unplaced others. Today Jigsaw and I were in for a delightful surprise: as we stood well down the row, the judge approached cautiously and presented us with a vast green and purple rosette with '8th' emblazoned across the middle.

Trailing clouds of glory, with the rosette adjusted for maximum effect, we headed home. We paused at the terrier-racing ring to watch the small dogs chase a rabbit-skin down the course. I'd never seen such raw competitive spirit. Trevor was beating all comers and was obviously going to win the bag of pigs' ears that were the victor's laurels. Frank leant against the fence, watching. "See the little fellow Trevor?" he asked, as he patted Jigsaw's neck, "I reckon he thinks that there rabbit-skin's on heat."

Sitting Targets

The problem of house-sitting in our village is a knotty one. Many of us have houses, and animals, that can't just be locked and left when we go away. Local teenagers could be persuaded to earn pocket money by house-sitting, but the sight of Colin's daughter (age 18), for instance, singing to her iPod while drifting among his animals and randomly feeding them does not inspire confidence.

So a few holidays ago we arranged for Jen, the primary school headmistress, to house-sit while we were away. There she planned her school strategies while dealing competently with anything I could throw at her – new guinea fowl chicks, our ancient whippet, vicious geese – and she never failed us. We always returned to a tidy house and happy animals. The snag was that even though her bill was modest, her services still tended to cost more than our holiday.

I was discussing the house-sitting dilemma with Anna, the postmistress, while Kay my next-door neighbour listened in. "I've had a brainwave," Kay said. "Why don't we house-sit for each other?" It was a suggestion of sheer genius.

My family was first to go on holiday. Kay waved us off happily and I felt a warm glow of satisfaction to think of our excellent plan. When we returned a fortnight later, she looked fraught. "Everything's fine," she said and left hurriedly. As we settled back in, niggling doubts began to fill my mind. Why were there sheep footprints in the rose beds? Why was Jigsaw, admittedly normally a chunky horse, now completely circular? And what was the strongly alcoholic smell that filled the kitchen? I knew that all these questions would be answered in time.

Sure enough, news of Kay's frantic stint at our house filtered back to me via the village shop, neighbours and from Kay herself. She had absent-mindedly left some gates open, and my animals had embraced their new-found freedom. Several people had witnessed the sheep's enjoyment of our garden and the vicar returned Jigsaw from her happy night in the churchyard during which she had eaten everything she could find. Finally, on the day we got back, Kay had returned from the garden centre where she had been replacing Jigsaw's depredations, to discover that she had turned the Aga up to melting heat by mistake during a bout of last-minute dusting. In the blast furnace of our kitchen, six bottles of homemade elderberry wine re-fermented, burst their corks and formed a sticky lake on the floor.

And now it was my turn, as Kay and her family were off to Italy. On the first morning of my shift I woke to the promise of a perfect summer's day. Encouraged, I pulled my wellies on over my pyjamas and went outside. The door clicked shut behind me just as I remembered that I'd need a key. I looked in at the sitting room window to see Kay's dog Humphrey staring back at me. He accurately assessed the situation, gave an excited bark and started to tear up a sofa cushion. As the room filled with feathers, I scrambled on to a low roof, via a water butt, climbed up and squeezed through the open bathroom window. Below me in the road I saw Colin, gazing open-mouthed, so news of my pyjama-clad attempt at cat burglary would soon be all over the village.

As things started, so they continued. Kay's pig made a bid for freedom and the whole village was alerted before she was spotted in the public bar of the Friendly Ferret. Humphrey shredded a wicker laundry basket and the cat unexpectedly had kittens. Finally, I found a swarm of small frogs swimming in the downstairs loo just as Kay's car turned into the driveway. I went home and called Jen. Next year I am leaving house-sitting to a professional. Funnily enough, Kay is in complete agreement.

The Power and the Glory

I was taking our dogs on their daily lap around the village when I came across my neighbour Frank nailing a poster to a telegraph pole. 'Steam Fair' it said in big, friendly letters, above an attractive picture of a traction engine, while promising, 'A Nice Day Out'. I was intrigued and questioned Frank further. Always happy to chat on any subject, he became voluble. Apparently the Steam Fair took place in the next village along and, among other attributes, could boast the finest collection of stationary engines in the area. In fact if I was interested Frank could show me his own personal stationary engine as a foretaste of the joy to come. "It's all of 1.5 horse power," he assured me.

Truthfully, I prefer horse power to be provided by real horses, but I couldn't spurn Frank's kind offer. Anyway, his wife Phyllis had baked a batch of courgette muffins that she was keen for me to try. After sampling the cakes, I accompanied Frank to an outbuilding where his engine was being groomed for the big event. He pulled some levers and then with a tremendous 'pop' it spat about a pint of bright green liquid from one tube into another. "Just look at that," said Frank with satisfaction, "you won't find engineering like this nowadays." As he started fussing around with an oily rag I took the opportunity to slip out and rejoin Phyllis in the kitchen. She wasn't too sure about the engine thing either.

But there was no escaping the Steam Fair. Everybody in the village seemed to be going and, as it was a beautiful day, I set out with Julia, the hedge fund manager, along the footpath that linked the two villages. We heard the fair well before we saw it and as we came out of the woods the noise of whirring engines hit us, as did a most distinctive aroma of steam, oil and crushed grass. The place was heaving, and tents filled the neighbouring fields.

I found Frank and Phyllis behind a row of stationary engines, each one humming away obligingly. Frank was wearing his special flat cap for the occasion and demonstrating his pride and joy's perfections to a group of fellow enthusiasts. Phyllis seemed to have ditched her initial reservations and sat regally on a canvas chair to receive visitors, serving them tea with yet more courgette muffins.

I spied another neighbour, Colin, beaming at a steam threshing machine that did its business with terrific commotion, as an added bonus covering bystanders in a thick layer of dust. He yelled something through the racket, and I could just about distinguish the words: 'magnificent' and 'watch it all day'. I was obviously missing something.

A mighty circular saw was drawing a crowd to match. With raw power and a refreshing disregard for health and safety, it noisily sawed an entire tree trunk into chunks. Everybody applauding was covered in oil and sawdust. My fellow villagers were everywhere, and I witnessed some sights to treasure: Colin, rigid with importance, driving slowly around the main ring on an ancient and obviously cherished tractor. Julia asking for a 'medium-rare' burger and then being given a bap filled with something that could only be described as 'very well done'.

Mr Addington in his favourite role as car-park attendant nearly coming to blows with a local celebrity who desired a ringside parking space, whereas Mr Addington considered that he could line up with everybody else. The celebrity won eventually, but only after the President of the Steam Fair had been called, Mr Addington had been persuaded to get up from his recumbent position in front of the celebrity's shiny four-wheel drive, and everybody had gone off for a soothing drink.

And I finally got it. As a steam organ mangled music hall tunes, traction engines hissed and vintage cars paraded in the ring, my scepticism vanished into the warm summer air and I realised that this was yet another face of rural England, one that wears a boiler suit and enjoys the sound of a piston. The Steam Fair was a joyous step back in time that gave me, and the happy crowd all around, exactly what it said on the poster: A Nice Day Out.

All the Fun of the Fayre

Every year our village stages a summer show in Maurice the farmer's Home Field. It is called the 'Country Fayre', although many of us wish it wasn't. Apart from the dodgy spelling, the event is more in the nature of a 'Village Gathering', organised by the village and for the village, and outsiders are not particularly encouraged. But no one can face the multiple committee meetings that changing the time-honoured name would require, so 'Country Fayre' it is.

This summer the forecast had been cautiously optimistic but everybody installed weather protection, just in case. By the day of the Fayre, the Home Field resembled a shanty town of gazebos and garden umbrellas, so of course the sun shone down hotly throughout.

The Fayre changes slightly from year to year, but some things are perennial. Frank's ferrets are always there, enjoying the opportunity to writhe sinuously through drainpipes. Another cast-iron certainty is the line of village elders sitting on a row of straw bales and studying new arrivals closely. They are noting the best village cooks bringing their contributions to the food tent and observing the food containers they use, so they will know which quiche to choose when lunch arrives.

Everybody is encouraged to do their bit, and my contribution this year was to help run the raffle. This is really the annual recycling of unwanted Christmas presents kindly donated by the villagers, with a fruit basket from the Farm Shop added as Top Prize. The tickets for the assembled pile of fruit-scented candles, hand-knitted bobble hats and novelty books sold well under my stewardship, so I was able to hand over to Rachael the churchwarden with a clear conscience and set about exploring the Fayre.

Colin had requisitioned the bottom half of the field for his chosen activity of fly casting into plastic hoops. I arrived to uproar. Ben, casting without due care and attention, had let his line flick against the back of Mrs Addington's thick tweed skirt as she passed by. Ben's happy cries of, "I've won! I've caught a Chub!" didn't help the ensuing commotion one bit. I fled to the food tent, arriving just in time to see Bodger, Ben's jolly Labrador, being escorted firmly out. It transpired that Bodger had followed his nose on arrival and headed straight for lunch. There he had polished off three quiches before being ejected. Luckily he hadn't reached the best of the bunch, baked by Joan, the vicar's wife. The remaining quiches now formed the centre of an animated group of villagers, loading their plates before any further disaster befell.

The high point of the afternoon was the prize-giving. Colin's daughter Annabel, currently on her gap year, was back in the village briefly in between teaching at a Ugandan orphanage and backpacking through Peru. It turned out that she could also cook like an angel and had swept the board. Julia, who expected to win 'Victoria Sponge Cake', and Audrey who usually carried off the honours for 'Jams and Jellies', were momentarily tight-lipped, but their better natures reasserted themselves and they gave in with good grace to the triumphant march of youth. In fact the only class Annabel hadn't won was 'Basket of Summer Vegetables', which always went to one of the Anderson brothers, the other brother reliably coming second. In previous years, whichever brother won usually cast aspersions on the other's entry, which resulted in a punch-up. This year the judges cunningly pre-empted the row by giving the brothers joint first prize, so all was harmony. But the overall victor's laurels went to Annabel, who told the assembled villagers that winning the champion's cup was, like, epic.

After the prize-giving was over, and Annabel had left with a flick of hair and a gleam of midriff to tell her friends all about it on Facebook, it was time to tidy up. We collected our gazebo and set off home. I looked back at Maurice's rapidly emptying field and reflected that once again our Country Fayre had indeed been, to borrow a phrase, epic.

Julia's prize winning Victoria Sponge cake recipe

110g (4oz) caster sugar
110g (4oz) butter (room temperature)
110g (4oz) self-raising flour
2 large eggs

Organisation is vital when it comes to baking a prize winning sponge cake. Before I start, I really make a point of properly instructing my wonderful housekeeper Irene to purchase and assemble the following ingredients:

Irene likes to feel involved, so I allow her to mix the sugar and butter in a food processor until it is fluffy and pale. Then she adds the eggs one at a time and mixes them well in, scraping the sides of the processor with a spatula as necessary. Finally she adds the flour and mixes it lightly with about 5 short bursts of the food processor.

Then Irene spreads the cake mixture carefully and evenly in two greased and floured 18cm (7 inch) cake tins which she places in the centre of the oven at 170 degrees (gas mark 3).

I have many calls on my time so I'm usually achieving things somewhere else when the moment arrives for the cake tins to come out. Therefore I entrust Irene to wait for about 25 minutes, until the sponge cakes are golden brown and springy to the touch. Then she takes them out of the oven and carefully turns them onto a wire rack to cool.

Presentation is vital with a competition cake, so I brief Irene in advance to fill the cake layers with fresh whipped cream and her delicious home-made strawberry jam, and to sift a pretty layer of icing sugar over the top.

Then I simply place the completed Victoria Sponge on a pre-prepared cake plate with doily (thank you Irene), take it to the village Country Fayre and enter it in the Victoria Sponge class. And then I win it (apart from the year that Colin's daughter Annabel took part. Coincidentally I have organised a summer internship for Annabel next year that sadly means she won't be able to compete in the Country Fayre). Of course Irene has a full schedule of domestic duties back in my beautiful home, so cannot come and applaud my triumph.

People are amazed that I find time for successful competitive cake baking, year after year. But as the saying goes: "if you want something done, ask a busy woman!"

September

Ploughing on

The village ploughing match was rapidly approaching and excitement was reaching fever pitch. This meant that if two people met in the village shop, one was highly likely to say, "It's the ploughing match soon," and the other was almost certain to reply, "Yes, so it is." We take our pleasures steadily in these parts.

Our contribution to the event was to drive through the chilly pre-dawn to collect the key player in the hog roast that was an intrinsic part of the festivities. Our local, the Friendly Ferret, was providing the hog roaster, and the hog awaited us in the pub fridge. Somebody had kindly removed its head and tail and threaded it neatly onto a pole, which was a relief. We loaded hog and roaster into the trailer and drove back to Maurice's farm, where the match was about to begin.

Tractors were arriving in a steady stream, despite the early hour. They sat majestically on the back of trailers driven by farmers and fanatics, with a sprinkling of keen amateurs. While the enthusiasts buffed up the paintwork of their darlings before going to do battle, the hog refused to co-operate. It assumed a starfish position with splayed legs, and jammed the roaster. A small crowd collected and stared with fascinated horror as the parts of the hog that were not raw pig started to burn sooty black. My husband produced some bailer twine from his pockets and tied its legs back together. The mechanism started up, the hog revolved and everyone relaxed.

Back on the sun-baked stubble, a horse had arrived. This was not just any horse, this was 17 hands of glossy magnificence, with long white legs and a handlebar moustache. The bystanders immediately divided into Mars and Venus. Mars stayed faithful to the tractors, while Venus rushed to adore the horse, who was called Sheriff.

Our hog was still making its presence felt. The bailer twine burned to a frazzle, releasing the hog's legs, which jammed the roaster again. My neighbour Frank appeared. "I'll fettle him!" he said and produced some wire. The hog nearly fettled Frank when its legs twanged apart in his grasp, and sprayed him liberally with hot fat. Red-faced and smarting, Frank finally bested the hog and wired it back into a suitable shape. Through a gap in the tent I could see another villager, Ben, roaring proudly past in a huge tractor. "Ben's got a five-furrow reversible plough," said Frank, admiringly. The mighty equipage headed down the field and commenced ploughing. Suddenly there was a loud bang, a shout from Ben, and his tractor stopped moving. Leaving his machinery stranded, Ben strode back up the field. "Poor Ben," said Frank mournfully, "he's broken his bottom link!" Ben then disappeared into the beer tent, surrounded by well-wishers. It obviously wasn't hurting him too much.

Sheriff set off down the field, all enormous hooves and clanking chains, encouraged by cheerful shouts from his brawny woman handler. His plough scraped a very shallow very slow furrow. I wouldn't have admitted it to the Sheriff fan-club, but I suddenly saw the point of tractors.

Colin was a vintage tractor enthusiast and turned up wearing a pink cravat, a serious expression and a sweatshirt with a picture of a tractor on the front. His tractor was Sheriff's main rival for the crowd's affections. "That Colin's got a Field Marshall!" breathed Frank, and gave up hog roasting duties immediately to go and join the crowd of worshippers.

Against the backdrop of a tiny blue tractor with orange wheels pulling Ben's huge machine off to be repaired, Anna the postmistress presented the prizes. Onlookers were well equipped with mugs of tea and pork rolls, the hog having finally given in finally given in gracefully. In the evening sun, the field behind us looked like an eccentric patchwork quilt. I could see Maurice in the distance. He was beginning to plough Sheriff's single furrow, Colin's obsessively straight furrows, and all the day's activity back into the unassuming corduroy flat bed from which would spring his peerless barley next year.

The Bartering Business

My first brush with the fine art of bartering, as practised by our village, occurred soon after we moved in. We'd already had the welcoming ceremony, when villagers introduced themselves with a gift of biscuits or a pot plant and improved those first whirlwind days out of all recognition. Now there was a ring on the doorbell and Frank, a close neighbour, appeared with some onions. "Thought you could do with these," he said, pressed them into my hands, and departed. How kind! And how kind of Maurice, the farmer, to bring us carrots. And how very kind of Rachael, the churchwarden, to present me with a bag of borlotti beans and a list of services.

All was explained when Mrs Addington arrived on the doorstep with a cauliflower. As I exclaimed at her thoughtfulness, and my joy that we had chosen such a welcoming place to live, she interrupted me. "Yes, well. I'm sure you will remember us come asparagus season!" With these cryptic words she left, leaving me to do some rapid thinking. I realised that yes, the village was being kind, but not in a disinterested way. They expected a return for their vegetables, and that return appeared to be asparagus.

The army quarters I had lived in until then had many fine points, but opportunities for luxury vegetable growing hadn't been among them. I turned to my books, where I discovered the unfortunate truth about the undergrowth we'd strimmed to make our hen run. I rushed out to see if anything could be salvaged, and some contented hens looked up from what I now knew to be the ruins of a cosseted long-standing asparagus bed. Luckily time was on my side – I feverishly encouraged my new herb garden. When the asparagus season arrived I could fend off criticism with bunches of herbs and fine brown eggs.

As time progressed, I was admitted to the second circle of bartering: preserves. The same etiquette applied – if you shared your surplus in a time of plenty, you could expect a good return. But there must be a fair exchange. I will long remember the expression on Colin's face when a newcomer – fresh from 'the City' – offered a muddy swede (a vegetable loathed in these parts) in exchange for Colin's sumptuous sweetcorn. By the same token, you learn that if Audrey gives you a pot of Seville marmalade with meticulously hand-cut peel, it's a bad idea to palm her off with some of your runny green tomato chutney with the strangely metallic aftertaste.

And so I moved onto the third circle of bartering, in which produce is exchanged for services. I could now ask Frank to feed my hens while I was on holiday, and he would help himself to eggs while I was away. This worked so well that I agreed to water Colin's tomatoes in return for access to his crop. I was totally unprepared for the true glory of a sun-warmed prime tomato and after a blissful fortnight of gorging on them, I realised that Colin was almost due back and his vines were stripped. Panic! I was just planning to buy some replacements and somehow tie them to the vines when mercifully the mix of sun and extreme amounts of tomato food worked their magic. By the time Colin returned there was a respectable showing of tomatoes, and I had learned another bartering lesson: moderation.

Now, after several years in the village, I am an integral part of a complex web of bartering. Although not a gifted cook, I can do birthday cakes. So when Maurice asked me if I would make a fairy-tale castle cake for his daughter's birthday, I assented with pleasure. Maurice in turn released a squad of his goslings to Colin, who will give Rachael some tennis lessons. Rachael will donate some exotic vegetables to Audrey, who has an unused horse rug which she will pass on to my cob, Jigsaw, who has a gap in her wardrobe. And (this is the really good bit) no money will change hands at any stage. Practically perfect!

Off the Beaten Track

Mr and Mrs Addington's announcement that they intended to revive our village's moribund Rambling Club met with a muted response. My neighbours and I have no problem with the concept of walking, we just prefer to walk for a reason: to get to the post office or exercise the dog. But to walk 12 miles on a precious Saturday morning on an organised ramble? With the Addingtons? We needed convincing.

And the Addingtons did just that. They talked movingly about the health benefits of regular rambles, opportunities for social bonding, and furthering our knowledge of the local ancient landscape. They waxed lyrical about the joys of a tramp through dewy fields, plucking blackberries as we went. It worked. Rather to our surprise, more than 20 of us gathered outside the Addingtons' house one chilly Saturday morning, ready to head for the hills. Ben, who always likes to extract the maximum amusement out of any given situation, had opted to wear empire-building shorts with knee-length red socks. An outsize map case hung from his neck and he'd slung several enamel mugs around his person, which clattered as he walked. Colin, our pro, had two hiking poles, a daypack and a keen expression, but the rest of us wore a strange assortment of sports kit, wellies and coats, accessorised with children and dogs. Taken collectively, we were not a pretty sight.

The Addingtons emerged in correct rambling gear, and Mrs Addington gave a resigned sigh when she saw our motley crew. "Oh well. Mr Addington will lead today's walk. We have planned a very interesting route to the site of a Roman villa." And they strode off rapidly with the rest of us trailing along behind to the clinking sound of Ben's mugs. As we took to the fields, Mr Addington cleared his throat: "On our left are the remains of a medieval ridge and furrow system," he said importantly. Maurice, the farmer on whose land we were walking, looked confused. "No, that's Mum's old asparagus beds," he said. But Mr Addington wasn't hearing dissenting voices. Nor was he interested in pausing to allow villagers to help children over stiles, reclaim dogs from streams or pick mushrooms. He marched tirelessly onwards.

The route became more overgrown, as we shed coats and jumpers in the strengthening sun. We had now abandoned a well-marked footpath, pushed our way through a thicket and entered what looked like primeval forest. It was when we were crawling, single file, under a low bridge that Mrs Addington finally cracked. "Wallace!" she said sharply. We all stopped, fascinated. So that was his first name! He looked round enquiringly. "We are going the wrong way," stated his wife. "Nonsense, dear," he replied and plunged forwards, to be halted by an impenetrable wall of brambles. There ensued an enduring and entertaining row in icy undertones.

Mrs Addington won and immediately led us back to the sanity of the footpath. Having established her authority she turned doggedly in the correct direction for the Roman site. But some of us held back, scratched, hungry and disinclined for further rambling. And this is where Ben came into his own. Showing surprising proficiency with a compass, he plotted a direct route to our local pub and guided us unhesitatingly back to civilisation.

The Friendly Ferret welcomed us with open arms, and we were soon toasting the Rambling Club with Ben's enamel mugs. Some hours later the hard-core ramblers returned to the village, hot and weary. We watched as Mrs Addington distributed quiz sheets and her voice came clearly in through the open pub windows: "Now we shall see who has really been concentrating". Ben shuddered and hid behind his map case.

However, I am glad to report that despite a difficult beginning, our Rambling Club looks set to flourish. Ben has volunteered to lead the next walk – which will be shorter, on waymarked routes and will involve a pub. There's already plenty of interest. Though not from the Addingtons.

A Warm Welcome

Whenever I spot a removal van decanting its cargo into a recently sold property in our village, I am drawn to it like an iron filing to a magnet. Will the newcomers be nice? People to share a summer barbecue with, or to join for energising dog walks on frosty winter mornings? And I remember our own arrival in the village, fresh from years in army quarters, wondering whether we would be rejected as aliens or be included in the community.

We needn't have worried. Our quiet lane was soon filled by a throng of neighbours bearing gifts, all watched with benevolent interest by the neighbouring dairy herd. Soon we became the delighted owners of a cornucopia of bunched garden flowers and bundled garden produce. Soon afterwards we visited the local shop where Anna the postmistress introduced us to everybody in the vicinity, then went for a drink at the Friendly Ferret, where Ed the publican introduced us to everybody Anna had missed. We were in!

In fact, our village is big on inclusion, and newcomers make soft targets. You wake up one morning and realise that, without knowing quite how it happened, you are a Parochial Church Councillor, Friend of the Village Hall, Patron of the Lubbly Jubbly Playgroup and have promised to judge the tulip class at the next village flower show.

The kindly interest of your new community can be a great help in unexpected ways. My neighbour Frank was leaning on the wall, soon after my arrival, watching me dig out a herb garden. "Ah," he said appreciatively, "nice bit of soil there. That's where the people before you buried their cats." I stopped digging. "Yes," Frank carried on, "must be 50 years' worth of cats in there. They had a little woolly dog, too..." Suffice to say I found somewhere else for my herbs.

In village life you reap what you sow. I relish the thought that we are now surrounded by neighbours who support us in

time of need, just as we assist them. My neighbours have helped me round up escaped sheep, pep up our broadband connection and repair a cable nibbled through by our indoor rabbit (which left him miraculously unscathed but cut off all our power). In turn, I have piled up sandbags during a flood, assisted at kunekune pig hunts and most recently rescued my dignified neighbour Colin from the boot of his 4x4, in which he had become mysteriously child-locked. Letting him out was easy, doing it without falling over laughing was impossible.

Of course, some like their own space and prefer to enjoy rural peace without the complications of community life. Their position, once made clear, is respected. However time changes many things and the man who shuts his door firmly on carol singers when he first arrives may mellow and eventually find himself carolling in the cold with the rest of us. Mrs Addington's first act when she arrived in the village was to reject Frank's welcoming present of eggs from his Marans, stating that she did not care to feed upon the bodies of the unborn. From this unpromising beginning she has become a village stalwart.

I, in my turn, have now become one of the unofficial 'meeters and greeters'. Recently a cottage in the village changed hands and, seizing a jar of homemade chutney, I set off to introduce myself. The door opened on an immaculate couple who greeted me with friendliness but gazed with horror at my offering. Although it was my best plum chutney, I have to admit that it resembled the sort of specimen kept in a locked cupboard in the school biology lab. Six weeks later they were gone and the cottage was up for sale. Rumour had it that they had moved to Shropshire due to an unexpected promotion, but I knew better. They had been chased away by chutney. I still feel rather guilty about that.

Maurice's apple suggestions

September is apple month for me. My orchard is a beautiful place to be in right now, with all the apples hanging on the boughs and smelling just lovely in the sun. We've got some gnarled old trees that have been provisioning my family and the neighbourhood for generations. They've all got a story, mind you: my grandfather planted the 'Bloody Ploughman' as a tribute to Frank's grandfather, who worked for him all his life. Here are some of my favourites that should be ready to pick, and suggestions for serving them.

Bloody Ploughman, Cox's Orange Pippin, Lord Lambourne, Worcester Pearmain. *Eat freshly picked, with a chunk of cheese, crusty bread and homemade chutney. Or peel, core, and slice them, spread them out on a wire tray and dry for about 24 hours in the bottom of the Aga or the lowest setting of your cooker. Packed in zip-lock bags or frozen, they'll make a lovely snack.*

Arthur Turner, Peasgood Nonsuch, Reverend W Wilkes. *These boys are perfect for apple pie, apple crumble or a nice big baked apple filled with brown sugar, sultanas and a pinch of cinnamon.*

Ellisons Orange, James Grieve. *Juice them with a bit of lemon to stop the juice oxidising and turning brown.*

Foxwhelp, Morgan, Tom Putt: *My cider apples. Morgan is sweet and old Tom Putt, he's sharp.*

Windfalls. *I make fruit leather with these. Combine a basket of unpeeled windfalls cut into chunks, a punnet of blackberries and a jar of jam. Stew to a thick pulp. Sieve the pulp and spread in a thin layer onto baking trays lined with greaseproof paper. Dry out in the bottom of an Aga or at the lowest setting of your cooker for about three hours, though check this. When dry, cut into strips, dust with cornflour and store in a plastic storage box. Practice makes perfect, with fruit leather.*

October

Cooking up a Storm

A blustery wind blew me up the village street and into the relative calm of the post office. There I found Rachael, the churchwarden, excitedly explaining her latest money-earning venture to Anna, the postmistress. She had signed up with a cookware firm called 'The Coddled Egg' and would demonstrate their amazing range of products in people's own homes, thus making herself some money while still being there for Tabbie and Maddie, her two little girls. Anna and I listened with a degree of resignation – since Tabby's birth Rachael has made enthusiastic but short-lived attempts to train as a dental nurse, a driving instructor and a proof reader, all with the same idea in mind.

But we made supportive noises as Rachael told us about her first booking, at her sister Lucy's house in Dorset, where she would display her new wares to best advantage by cooking a goat's cheese soufflé followed by a gooey chocolate cake. What (asked Rachael buoyantly) could possibly go wrong?

I bumped into Rachael a week later, and she explained that her first cookware demo hadn't gone quite as planned. She'd put the soufflé in the Aga and was in full swing with her patter when a hideous truth became apparent. The Aga had run out of oil, its temperature was sinking fast, and so was Rachael's soufflé. At this tricky moment, Lucy's husband had appeared, and they had a frank exchange of opinions about exactly who was in charge of ordering domestic fuel. Rachael tried to distract the audience from the argument by producing the gooey chocolate cake, but she couldn't part it from its special container without the Aga's heat. Her increasingly frenzied attempts to unglue it certainly held people's attention, but she felt her first demonstration hadn't been entirely professional.

However, much like the gooey cake, Rachael was resilient. "How about you hosting a demonstration?" she asked. And, of course, I booked one. On the evening in question, Rachael turned up flustered and late, as her baby had been slow to settle. She pressed a complicated piece of plastic into my hands. "Your hostess present. It's for dicing eggs. Or possibly mangoes." She turned to the assembled audience, "I'm going to cook quiche for you tonight," she promised winningly, "with salad". The weather was chilly and secretly we'd have preferred a pot roast with mounds of potatoes, but we smiled encouragingly while she got to work.

The antibacterial pastry board was a success and the grater/cheese collection box coped manfully with the mounds of cheese that Rachael keenly grated into it. Trouble came with the salad. "You put your tomato into the Tomato Wizard, give it a quick twist and voila!" A dribble of tomato juice came out of the bottom of the Tomato Wizard, followed by gobbets of mangled tomato, which had to be painstakingly dug out with a skewer. Rachael tried again and a jet of red juice shot out of the side of the Wizard, scoring a direct hit on her snowy white Coddled Egg apron. Julia, the hedge fund manager, could bear it no longer and offered to take over tomato preparation. Rachael handed her the Tomato Wizard with relief and Julia grasped the device firmly. She gave it a deft twist and the tomato fell into two decorative halves. "Lovely," said Julia, "I'll order one of those."

The demonstration reached its climax with dessert – custard tartlets, which sat in their guaranteed non-stick tray. "I'll just flip them out," said Rachael, and whacked the tray on the underside. The tartlets zoomed upwards and my Labradors, who had been asleep in their baskets, suddenly realised that the air was full of custard. They made the most of this manna from heaven and, despite my best attempts, not a single tartlet was saved.

Rachael dropped by a few weeks later. As a result of good sales from my party, I had earned another present. She handed me a smooth granite rectangle. "It's a useful baking stone," she explained, "but actually I've given up the Coddled Egg franchise. A friend is importing ethnic jewellery from Namibia, and I want to get in on it!" and she departed, full of new plans. But the baking stone has indeed been useful. It's up at the top of the garden, reverently marking the final resting place of our much loved and sadly departed whippet.

A Chicken-and-Egg Situation

About now my Pekin bantams make a committee decision to stop laying eggs. Eggs are never top of their agenda anyway. They come under 'any other business' and the resolution to stop laying them is passed by unanimous vote. When Spring returns, other breeds start churning eggs out by the barrowload. My Pekins may (after due consideration) produce one perfect egg. Between the five of them. And there they will leave it until one of them feels like laying again, which may be some time. Eggs, to my little flock of portly dilettantes, are a privilege and not a right.

When a vague longing for a home produced omelette first crystallised into a desire to own hens, I didn't know where to start. The countryside may be clucking with poultry, but how to access it? I'd recently visited a farm park that had several poultry arks among its attractions and might have surplus. I rang up to enquire and was told they had a cockerel and a hen that they could spare. I sped over there, overjoyed at the thought of hen ownership just around the corner. But the cockerel they offered me was a Transylvanian Naked Neck and the hen was a Sicilian Buttercup. He looked like a scaled-down vulture. She had a complicated comb arrangement and a neurotic glare. I drove home even faster, and still without hens.

I found an advertisement in the local paper. 'Hens', it stated tersely, '£5 each'. Following directions, I drove into what looked like primeval forest, though it was actually quite close to Swindon. I fought my way past a tangle of brambles to a front door and knocked. The door swung open and a man with a grizzled ponytail, a magnificent paunch and waders looked at me expressionlessly. "I've come about the hens," I said tentatively. He ushered me into a wire compound and disappeared inside a shack. I heard frenzied squawks and he reappeared with two hens dangling upside-down from his fists. "Got 'em off their eggs!" he said triumphantly. I couldn't find the words to say I didn't want his thin brown hens, so I gave him a crumpled tenner and fled.

My new hens scarpered as soon as I put them in the run, and for the next fortnight watched me with swivelling eyeballs. I think that we could have made friends eventually, but it was not to be. An enterprising fox worked out one afternoon that he could dig under the fence. He invited friends and family in for a party, and I was henless again.

I buried the chicken wire all around the run and bought a smallholders' magazine containing a list of breeders. A specialist in Brahmas lived nearby. Brahmas are gorgeous – huge birds with feathery trousers and a massive nobility. I brought a cockerel and two hens home in triumph. As I introduced them to their new accommodation I felt like a hotel manager showing inadequate bedrooms to polite but disapproving VIP guests. My Brahmas had to duck their heads to enter the hen house, and quickly scratched up the hen run until it resembled a Hubble photograph of Venus. Although they laid plenty of eggs, I had to face it: they were just too big. I gave them to a friend with a huge fox-proof garden.

So it was back to the drawing board. What did I actually want from hens? And what did hens want from me? I could now offer a medium-sized ark in a secure run, with plenty of companionship and TLC. In return I hoped for cheerful, friendly hens who could provide enough eggs to make the odd spaghetti carbonara. And then I discovered my Pekin bantams, who do pretty much all of it. And if I sometimes have to slide furtively into the farm shop to top up on eggs, it's a price worth paying for the joy they bring in so many other ways. They do supply fine raw ingredients for spaghetti carbonara, too. In the summer months. Sometimes.

The Parish Plan

It was Mr Addington who came up with the suggestion of a 'Village Strategy'. He has a well-ordered mind and finds life here a little unstructured so, inspired by a visit to friends who were busily drawing up an ambitious future vision for their own village, he was brimming with zeal for controlled community empowerment back home. He organised a working party to put up a marquee, provided some plastic cups of wine (he knows us too well) and produced a keen man with rectangular spectacles who gave a motivational talk on the importance of the collective voice, then distributed flow charts and spreadsheets and departed.

We milled around the marquee, gazing bemusedly at the flow charts, finishing off the wine and using our collective voice to chat about the recent weather and its effect on our vegetable patches until Julia, the hedge-fund manager, took charge. Having persuaded us back to our seats, she invited suggestions from the floor for new facilities that might improve village life. After a slow start, these came thick and fast. We settled on some workable proposals to be explored by sub-committees, the results to be presented at a second meeting.

I found myself on the Pavements subcommittee with Rachael, the churchwarden, and Frank. We met on the only village road without grass growing up the middle, ready to study traffic flow. After a long wait, the distant whine of an over-revved engine was heard and Ralph, our oldest inhabitant, drove his little red car up the hill. As we watched, the postman came from the other direction and Ralph swerved unhesitatingly into the hedge to avoid him. He continued on his mission to the Friendly Ferret for his lunch-time pint with one wing mirror wreathed in old man's beard and spindleberries: there was no doubt that a pavement would have severely cramped his style. Next along was the milk tanker, which filled the road from hedge to hedge leaving no room for a possible pavement. We didn't spot any pedestrians, but our network of footpaths allows folk to take a direct cross-country route rather than walk along the roads. We concluded that our vision for the village's future probably didn't include pavements.

At the village shop Anna, the postmistress, revealed the findings of her Bus Shelters sub-committee. Currently the bus stops outside the home of Maurice the farmer, and anyone waiting for a bus is welcomed inside for a cup of tea, especially if it is cold or rainy. Nobody showed much enthusiasm to change this routine, least of all Maurice's elderly mum June, who liked the company.

Julia, head of the Play Park sub-committee, was also in the shop and co-opted the rest of us to consider the provision of a new play area for the community. The school bus had recently dropped off the children who were loosely grouped around the mighty oak on the village green. Some were swinging on a low branch, others leaning against the trunk and chatting. A splinter group was jumping noisily into a heap of fallen leaves, while quieter types were using the stump of a fallen sister-tree as a plinth to re-create the living statues seen on shopping trips to Bath. "I think the village already has a play park," Julia said.

Mr Addington, as resident health and safety tsar, had been the obvious choice to head the Street Lighting sub-committee. He met Ben and Maurice one evening to discuss the issue. It was a clear night and Ben pointed out the Plough right above their heads. After some gentle wrangling as they attempted to identify Cassiopeia, Mr Addington rushed home to collect his battered copy of The Boy's Big Book of Planets and the sub-committee spent a happy half hour constellation-spotting. Later, in the Friendly Ferret, they concurred that the village's lack of light pollution more than made up for its lack of street lighting.

Our second meeting was short and to the point. The sub-committees presented their conclusions and everyone unanimously agreed that our village strategy, for the moment, is to keep our village exactly as it is. Even Mr Addington didn't object.

Service with a Smile

Now that I have resided in the village for some years, I've been allotted a small section of church windowsill on which to create a flower arrangement at significant festivals throughout the year. I received a reminder from Audrey, the local flower-arranging queen, telling me to bring my flowers to the church on the day before Harvest Festival (theme: 'Nature's Goodness'). I turned up as requested with the best flowers that my garden could provide, which wasn't saying much, bulked out with some ripe ears of barley. I completed my arrangement, and placed a ring of apples from the bent old tree in the orchard around the base of the vase. Then I froze as Audrey approached. She looked carefully at my efforts and then at me. "Well, Aly, that's…quite sweet!" she said, and continued on to those more worthy of her notice.

After Audrey and her entourage exited, I went up to the altar to admire the truly spectacular floral displays produced by the senior flower-arrangers. There was a rustling noise and the vicar emerged, peering over a stook of corn like a shy woodland creature. He was attempting to pile up some of the enormous marrows and pumpkins that the villagers donate so generously. "I hear that many town churches only receive packaged food offerings," he puffed as he heaved on a striped giant of a marrow. "Indeed, I think them most fortunate!"

Our vicar is a shining example of a good man of God, but he has his own particular style. On Harvest Festival day he entered the church with dignity, walked to the front and came to rest behind a small table. He peeled off his fingerless gloves with great ceremony and laid them on the table. Then he removed his spectacles and put them in their case. Finally, he turned his hearing aid off with a defiant click. This performance is watched with bulging eyes by newcomers to the village, but with affectionate resignation by the rest of us.

Now, stripped for action, he led the opening prayers, finishing each one half a sentence behind everybody else. Then it was time for Joan, his wife, to make her presence felt. "I've found some rather good new words to our first hymn, which will make much more sense to our younger members. You'll find the words on a sheet in your hymn books," she said with an enthusiastic smile. And the hymn began. "We plough the fields with tractors!" sang the congregation obediently, while the vicar roared, "We plough the fields and scatter!" And so it continued for the rest of the hymn – the modernists faithful to Joan, the traditionalists loyally following the vicar's lead.

The service continued along its familiar path until it was time for communion. Rachael, who has a busy time combining the duties of motherhood and church warden, clapped her hand to her mouth. "Oh no! I've forgotten the communion wafers!" she hissed and rushed to the back of the church. We listened with interest to the rummaging noises coming from the vestry and a wail of "The wine's empty, too!" The vicar, noticing the disturbance, switched his hearing aid back on and smiled benignly: "God moves in mysterious ways," he said. Rachael reappeared with some substitutes she had collected from the ploughman's lunches, spread on the table at the back of the church for the congregation to enjoy later.

I am proud to report that the hurriedly sanctified rosemary focaccia with which communion was memorably celebrated at Harvest Festival this year came from my breadmaker. It went very nicely with Colin's 'fruity little Merlot', and almost made up for the sad fact that I am, and probably always will be, rubbish at flower-arranging.

Kay's spooktastic pumpkins

Halloween is such a great time of year for my kids! First we get hold of a pumpkin. Len Anderson grows the best pumpkins around here but he's a bit funny about parting with them. So I chat with Len at the gate while Cosmo, Milo and Ludo nip around the back and grab the biggest pumpkin they can see. It's OK, they leave a tenner in the gap in the pumpkin leaves. Then we make a run for it

When we've got our pumpkin safely home we do the fun stuff. First of all we make a **jack-o'-lantern**:

- Cosmo uses a sharp, serrated knife to cut off the lid. He cuts away from himself, because trips to A&E are really boring
- Milo uses a spoon to scoop out the seeds and things
- Ludo draws a face on the pumpkin with a marker pen and then cuts out eyes, nose and mouth. Straight lines are best, and he puts in loads of big scary teeth!
- Then we put a tea light inside it, replace the lid and put it outside on the wall to welcome in other kids for apple-bobbing!

There's loads of yummy things you can do with the pumpkin's insides

Roast pumpkin seeds. Rinse seeds, remove stringy bits. Pat dry, then toss in olive oil and salt (to taste). Spread evenly on an oiled baking tray and roast at 170 degrees for about half an hour, turning them every ten minutes. Check to make sure they don't burn and take them out when they're golden brown. Epic!

Pumpkin soup. Fry two chopped onions in oil for about 5 minutes. Add about 1kg pumpkin flesh, cut into chunks, and cook for a further 10 minutes, stirring occasionally. Pour 1litre of vegetable stock into the pan and simmer for 10 minutes or until the pumpkin is soft. Blend until smooth then add salt and pepper to taste plus a small tub of cream. Sooper!

November

Cinema Paradiso

I'm not sure who started the village film club. Possibly the Addingtons, who constantly strive to raise the local arts profile. Possibly hedge-fund manager, Julia, also a devotee of civilised pursuits. Certainly not Colin, who was briefly trapped in the village hall at a recent dance workshop organised by Julia. Enticed by the word 'workshop', he had wandered in searching for power tools and routers and found himself being encouraged to explore his relationship with nature through interpretative dance. He beat a horrified retreat and now shunned the arts. And not me, whose cinematic comfort zone is set firmly between the latest James Bond and Mamma Mia.

The film club met monthly and watched mainly independent films on a large screen funded by a community grant. The monthly advertisement in the parish magazine billed

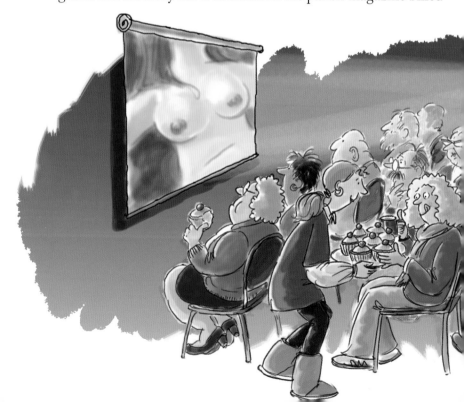

the films on offer as 'challenging' or 'disturbing', and I had no difficulty in finding pressing engagements that left me unable to attend each screening.

That was until I was in the post office shop, admiring a display of meringues. They were obviously home baked to a very high standard. "Noreen made those," said Anna the postmistress, proudly. "You know, Steve's wife. Steve's the projectionist for the film club, while Noreen makes lovely cakes and serves them there." Really? My first flicker of interest in the film club stirred. Shortly afterwards I was chatting to Rachael, the churchwarden. "I'm going to the film club tomorrow," she said. "You really should give it a try. They're showing a comedy this month, to see if it's more popular than the usual art-house fare." Cakes and a comedy! I decided to go.

There was an atmosphere of controlled panic when I turned up at the village hall the next evening. Steve was wrestling with something electronic behind a big blank screen, and the air was full of white noise. On the plus side, I spotted a pile of cake tins on a side table. Steve cleared his throat: "Sorry folks: this film's not going to work. But it's OK – we'll show next month's film instead. It's from the newly emerging Lithuanian film industry and is really thought-provoking."

As he started to set it up, I decided to vanish into the night. But then Noreen appeared at my elbow, and offered me a slice of carrot cake and a mug of tea. Wavering, I looked at the screen, which announced that the film would be subtitled. "I haven't brought my specs, I won't know what's going on!" I wailed. Mr Addington overheard me. "Aly, sit by me and I'll keep you in the picture!" My fate was sealed. I sat down resignedly next to him and demolished the delicious cake.

Meanwhile, two enormous faces were staring intently at each other on screen. "Vilius and Milda are questioning each other's intentions," Mr Addington whispered. Noreen, who obviously believed in keeping film-watchers well supplied, passed around a plate of cupcakes with pastel icing. They were superb. Back on the screen, the couple were getting along famously. Mr Addington ignored the cupcakes, absorbed by the uninhibited bedroom scene. I told myself that this was high art and therefore not embarrassing at all, and helped myself to another cupcake.

The action shifted to a seedy bar and things turned violent. "Their love is doomed," Mr Addington sighed. Fortunately Noreen chose this moment to circulate a mound of millionaire's shortbread, and its exquisite flavours, accompanied by a second cup of tea, kept me busy and happy despite the agonising events unfolding in front of me. Finally the camera panned out from a lone figure standing by a dark cross, which became more and more distant until it was lost in a huge horizon. Mr Addington, who had been too emotionally involved with the film to keep me up to speed with the plot, now wept silently into a white handkerchief. Noreen respectfully passed a tray of wickedly rich chocolate brownies around.

The film ended and the lights came up – the show was over. As I walked home, I found Julia standing still in the car park. "That film made me wonder...," she said quietly. I was wondering too, as to whether Noreen would share her cupcake recipe. The film club's next offering is billed as 'elliptical', and I will be there to watch it. Noreen is bringing her famous lemon drizzle cake. One way or the other, I'm looking forward to an excellent evening.

The Big Bang

Bonfire night brings annual chaos and confusion to our normally peaceful village. Three years ago, Maurice the farmer was about to light, ceremoniously, the mighty bonfire he had constructed on his land when a small hedgehog walked out of it. The rest of the evening was spent carefully dismantling the bonfire in case it held more hedgehogs. It didn't – the hedgehog turned out to be a lone wolf – but the anticlimax was acute. Two years ago, the bonfire Guy (made by Ben, the local joker) bore such an unmistakeable resemblance to Colin, one of our village elders, that even Colin noticed. Colin took offence and apologies were demanded but Ben was unrepentant: the row rankled for weeks. Last year, someone (suspicion hovers over Ben) doctored Maurice's special Bonfire Night punch, making it strong enough to fell a buffalo. This inflamed the simmering enmity between the Anderson brothers, who do most of the odd jobs in the village, and they brought their annual Christmas punch-up forward a month.

Then there is the delicate question of fireworks. The village is divided into two camps – those in favour see them as an enjoyable flourish of colour, light and noise against the encroaching darkness of winter. The anti-firework brigade has a different view – fireworks frighten the animals, cost too much and probably contribute to global warming. Last year the pro-firework lobby was in the ascendant, and every guest was expected to bring a handful of fireworks along with them to light up the night. But we gathered in the darkness in Maurice's field with a certain amount of trepidation.

The bonfire, checked thoroughly for wildlife, flared up and the anonymous Guy burned merrily. We stood around with glasses of punch (pre-sampled by Maurice) and waited for the fireworks. His dad was in charge of them this year, leaving Maurice free to dispense punch and indigestible sausages. He carefully lined up the first battery, lit the blue touch paper and retired. Off went the rockets and burst with a mighty flash and bang directly over the cottage nearby belonging to Ted – one of those who couldn't be doing with fireworks, and often said so loudly in the village shop. Maurice's dad, it was suddenly remembered, couldn't be doing with Ted, due to a trading of insults at school over 60 years ago. As his cottage was lit up like the centrepiece of an expensive laser show, Ted burst out of his front door and attacked the first target he could see.

This was a soft target. Quentin and Rosie, newcomers to the village, had been standing at the edge of the party smiling nervously and holding sparklers. Suddenly they were joined by a cross old man, who shouted at them in incomprehensible deepest Wiltshire. Their sparklers fizzled out as they tiptoed away. As it happened, this was the best thing that could have happened to them as far as village bonding went. Ben saw their predicament, scooped them up and dragged them into the middle of the revellers. Soon they were laughing, drinking incautious quantities of punch and vowing never to leave this lovely new village they'd been so fortunate to find.

Maurice yelled at his dad, who took umbrage and sent the next lot of fireworks straight up vertically. They looked terrific as they burst with cracks and pops directly above our heads, but then the inevitable happened and they came whizzing down again. The spent carcass of a firework hit the ground next to me with a reverberating thwack and I, along with most of the other guests, decided to watch the rest of the fun from underneath a large tree. Maurice and his dad stood firm, silhouetted by the blaze, as used fireworks rained down around their ears. Maurice's dad was still arguing defensively with his son when he set off the final barrage of rockets, and didn't notice as they zipped low through the branches of our sheltering tree. Twigs pattered down as, for the second time that night, everybody ducked, and ran.

Next morning I walked past the bonfire field where Maurice and his father were clearing up. They were pointedly ignoring each other as Ted, seated by his open window, called out unwanted advice and criticism. As I watched Maurice pull a couple of spent fireworks with visible effort from the exact place where my family had been standing the night before, it came to me: this Bonfire Night would go down in village history as The Year that Maurice's Dad did the Fireworks.

Murder Most Horrid

I was intrigued to receive an invite from Colin and Bridget to a murder mystery party. Although some of the old-school villagers, still yearn for formal dinner parties, most get-togethers in the village are casual verging on shambolic and we tend to prefer it that way. This event was different though – the theme was colonial Africa and I was told to arrive in the character of a hopeful young thing who had just been jilted. It sounded fun, and I accepted with alacrity.

I dropped in for a cup of tea on the afternoon of the party. Bridget was putting the finishing touches to a magnificently fluffy lemon mousse, an integral part of the plot. She had dressed the dining room to resemble the inside of a tent, with a revolving fan suspended from the roof and camp stools around the table. The room would be lit by oil lamps, and a computer played the sounds of a hot jungle night. The effect was magical, and I went home excitedly to dress in drooping florals and a pith helmet.

When we arrived, the party was in full swing. Mr Addington had made it plain that he wanted to be the police inspector who would identify and arrest the 'murderer' rather than the gouty colonel role he had been assigned, but he had given in gracefully and was wearing a fine pair of empire-building shorts that nearly came down to his ankles. Ben had interpreted his part as mining engineer by wearing a head torch and a bag marked 'High Explosives' and Peter, the vet, wore a vintage tropical policeman's uniform and was ignoring envious glances from Mr Addington. We were offered a plate of exotic starters by Colin (big game hunter and principal suspect) and the murder mystery began.

I was really getting into my role and sobbing noisily into a large khaki handkerchief, when Peter's bleeper went off. "Sorry, I'm on duty – must rush!" he said, and pausing to give his policeman's whistle, handcuffs and persona to a thrilled Mr Addington, he vanished into the night. Bridget rallied the table, and we continued with the plot. Then the phone rang and she went to answer it. Returning to the dining room, Bridget took stock of the table. Her party was going well, with everybody remembering who they were and saying their lines on cue. "I've just got to fetch Annabel from the station," she said. And with the unspoken thought, 'What could possibly go wrong?' she went to fetch her daughter.

What indeed? Ben decided to include Annabel's gerbil, Gavin, in the revelries and lifted him from his cage. Gavin, annoyed at being interrupted in the middle of his evening feast, fastened his teeth in Ben's thumb. A gory pas de deux ensued, with Ben and Gavin crashing around the dining room and covering a surprising number of surfaces with Ben's blood. Then Peter returned after a false alarm at the surgery. He went to reclaim his handcuffs and whistle, but Mr Addington wouldn't give them back. Both men glared at each other, meanwhile the computer got stuck on a loop of insanely high monkey shrieks. At which stage Bridget and Annabel returned from the station.

Bridget cast a disbelieving look at the party that she had left in such harmony and which was now arguing and bleeding to an unbearable backing track, and her jaw tightened as she looked for Colin, who had sidled into the kitchen. She separated Gavin from Ben's thumb and returned him to his cage, mopped up Ben and explained to Mr Addington that his role was pivotal to the evening. Then she tapped at the computer keyboard until it reverted to playing soothing ambient jungle noises.

Bridget took a deep breath. "Now," she said brightly, "who's for pudding?" And this is where her party really came unstuck. Because Colin, while lurking in the kitchen, had decided to 'help' and placed her lemon mousse in the Aga. It now resembled molten yellow rubber, with the final clue sealed hermetically inside. "Cream, anyone?" asked Colin, trying to pass off an awkward moment. It didn't work. Bridget turned on her husband with a snarl and it was evident that murder was going to be committed that night. And there was no doubt who would be the murderer – and the victim.

Back to the Wall

Jigsaw, my black-and-white cob, has a powerful personality and the physique of a killer whale. When she has an itch, her chosen scratching post had better watch out. With the subtlety of a dumper truck, she shouldered up to one of our dry stone walls and rubbed vigorously. The wall, weakened by years of neglect and Cotswold weather, promptly fell down. Jigsaw gazed smugly at the ruins lying at her ankles, shot me a glance that said: "Well, you'd better do something about that, then!" and ambled off to finish the job against her field shelter.

Each of our boundaries is marked by a dry stone wall, and this one was right by the road. I plugged the gap with a sheep hurdle and reviewed my options. It would cost an eye-watering sum to have the wall rebuilt by a professional. We could replace the wall with a stock fence, and yet dry stone walls are one of the glories of the area – field boundary, wildlife corridor and work of art combined. It was going to have to be self-help.

I joined a dry stone walling course at our local agricultural college, together with a motley crew of builders wanting to diversify and executives needing to de-stress. We spent a useful morning learning about health and safety ('avoid dropping stones on your toes – it hurts!'), then climbed into a mini bus and were trundled off to a long, ruinous wall. For the rest of the course we took down lengths of this wall and rebuilt it with great effort and ever-improving competence until (with arms stretched two feet longer and several missing fingernails) we earned our dry stone walling certificates.

I returned to our collapsed wall and soon had a fascinated audience consisting of Jigsaw (who felt a proprietary interest in the project) and a motley array of neighbours. The sight of me standing by the road in all weathers with my special walling hammer and a pile of stones proved irresistible to the casual onlooker, every one of whom was eager to share their stock of rural myths on the subject of dry stone walling.

First up was Mr Addington, who watched my efforts with a critical stare. "Did you know," he said, tapping my wall with a disapproving walking stick, "that this would originally have been built by skilled craftsmen? And they would have been paid a pound a mile. Now look at it!" I was doing my best, but was aware that my outfit of floral wellies, colourful raincoat and gardening gloves made me look anything but a skilled craftsman.

The wall was rising nicely when Frank, my near neighbour, popped his head over. Frank is a complete countryman and can turn his hand to most rural jobs. "I was doing a bit of walling once," he said, "and guess what I found in the wall I was working on? A hand! All the bones and all. Didn't know what to do with him, so I put him back in there and carried on." Yuk. "The old boys used to get paid a jug of ale a mile for walling once," he added. It was with a certain amount of trepidation that I took down the next chunk of wall but all it had to offer, besides stones, were some walnut shells left by an enterprising rat and an old horseshoe.

My wall was nearly finished when Colin came powering past with his rucksack, two titanium walking poles and Lycra shorts. "Can't stop," he said importantly, "I'm training for my walking holiday. Did you know it used to cost a penny a mile to build those things?" Yeah, right. I smiled weakly and levered the last topping stone into place. My wall wasn't perfect, but it wasn't bad either. All it needed was lichen to grow on it, and some wildlife to colonise it. I planted delicate threads of toadflax along the top and went inside.

The next morning I woke to a horrifying sight: Jigsaw was stress-testing my wall. Legs braced, lower lip flapping in ecstasy, she was massaging her broad bottom against it. She finished with a satisfied sigh, and swaggered off. But this time, the Cotswold limestone stood firm – the only casualty was the toadflax dangling limply from her tail. I felt a warm glow of satisfaction: not only had I done my bit towards preserving a distinctive part of the rural landscape, but I had provided Jigsaw with a robust leisure facility into the bargain. Result!

Mr Addington's notes on dry stone walling
(from a bystander's point of view)

As I stroll along our pleasant lanes, I often encounter a dry stone
waller mending one of the walls our parish is so liberally blessed
with. By careful study I have picked up a sound understanding of
requisites and practice of dry stone walling, and I am always happ
to pass on the benefit of my experience. Funnily enough I frequentl
notice a waller hiding behind the wall being constructed, or graspi
a hammer longingly, as I approach to instruct them in their craft.

Equipment required by the dry stone waller:

Waterproof coat (it will be raining), Hammer, Bucket, Length of stri
and a pair of wooden A frames, Gloves: here opinions differ. I
recommend use of gloves for hand protection, while my neighbour
Frank says only big girl's blouses use gloves when walling.

Equipment required by the dry stone walling observer:

Waterproof coat (it will be raining), Stout stick with which to poir
out irregularities in the wall under scrutiny

Building a dry stone wall

You simply disassemble the dry stone wall being worked on into it
component parts, construct a stout foundation and then, using man
tons of local stone, you build up the wall from both sides so that
separate walls are created, locked together with longer stones an
infilled with smaller stones. Each walling stone should be chock
to slope down from the centre to defect the rain. Then you just ca
off the wall with alternate large and smaller stones, a process
known locally as cock and henning. Some wallers use an A frame
length of string to ensure the wall is straight and some do it by

So as long as the waller possesses the strength of an ox, superio
hand/eye coordination, the soul of a craftsman and a lifetime's
experience, there is absolutely nothing complicated about the
art of dry stone walling.

December

A Christmas Carol

It never snows on Carol Singing night but it nearly always rains. Added to this, ours is a smallish village and the actual carol singers can be a bit thin on the ground. It is a delicate balancing act to have enough voices to make ourselves heard, while also leaving enough people at home to heat the mulled wine and line up the mince pies. So as we climbed into the trailer to be pulled around the village behind Maurice's tractor (fetchingly decorated with flashing fairy lights), our Christmas cheer needed a kick-start.

It didn't help that we started with the tougher gigs to get them over with, and it doesn't get tougher than the Addington household. We gathered in a shivering group outside their unlit porch and began singing Away in a Manger. Mr and Mrs Addington were out of their house like jack rabbits, closing the door firmly behind them and thus trumping the vicar's next move. Our vicar is a staunch man of God but he does feel the cold, and over the years has perfected a neat little trick. When a door was first opened, the vicar would stand uncomfortably close to whoever opened it, lantern upheld and an encouraging smile firmly in place. When they stepped back in alarm, he would say: "Are you sure? That is really most kind!" and we would surge into the house and start off on Hark! the Herald Angels sing before anyone could stop us. Happy minutes thawing out in a warm room, sampling some hastily assembled refreshments would almost invariably follow.

But the Addingtons were wise to this ploy. We stood outside in the rain while they listened intently to our efforts and then requested carols we didn't know. "Can we hear Adam Lay Ybounden? No? Oh dear. How about We Sing of a Mayden That is Makeles?" We just couldn't win. We gave them

Silent Night and pushed Angelina, Maurice's fairy-like little niece, forward with the collecting box. Mr Addington carefully inserted 20p. Angelina, who has total self-confidence, asked for more. It was not forthcoming.

Our next call was to a family recently arrived in the village. Would they shout at us and set their dogs on us? Or might they possibly invite us in for sausage rolls and a drink? We rang the front doorbell with the same spirit of anxious enquiry as somebody poking a tarantula with a small twig. And we struck gold. The new family invited us in, listened to our carols with every symptom of ecstatic enjoyment, plied us with refreshments and pushed a lovely crisp note into the collecting box. It was still raining and we were now sitting in puddles in the back of the trailer, but we didn't care – we were feeling festive.

Ben, whom we relied on for bass notes, began to show his partiality for a drop of mulled wine. As we continued the house calls and glass after glass was brought out for the singers, he availed himself continuously of what was on offer. Nemesis struck when we were singing one of our best carols in Anna the postmistress's home. "Gloria," Ben sang, "Gloria, Gloria, Gloria," his voice going deeper with each repetition until

he collapsed on the floor in a giggling heap. We supported him outside and levered him carefully back into the trailer to sleep it off.

Finally we reached journey's end: our local pub, the Friendly Ferret, which lived up to its name in every possible way. We crowded into the welcoming bar and raised the rafters with a final selection of our favourite carols. As the regulars listened, I gazed at the faces surrounding me. Happy, melancholy, relaxed, anxious or simply quite strange – each one of them a valued member of our little community. "We wish you a Merry Christmas and a Happy New Year!," we sang, and we meant every word.

That's Showbusiness

When I arrived in our village, I often heard about a wonderful pantomime staged some years previously. It had obviously given a great deal of pleasure, and whoever was telling me about it would end by saying: "Such a shame you weren't there, you'd have loved it!"

So I was among the first to sign up when I heard plans were afoot for another Christmas production, and a pantomime committee was hastily assembled. Maurice, full-time farmer and part-time devotee of amateur dramatics, was the driving force and supporting roles were doled out around the table. I was given the job of re-writing the script to reflect village life and bring exotic Aladdin (our panto of choice) closer to the home-grown audience. Maurice, as casting director, had been particularly successful. Some roles had practically cast themselves – Ben, the village joker was born to play Widow Twankey, and we were lucky that Colin's teenage daughter Annabel was currently at home and prepared to take the part of principal boy. But Maurice's biggest coup was persuading Mr and Mrs Addington, by much mention of symbolism and pre-Christian imagery, to appear as the pantomime cow.

The show slowly took shape. Maurice ceased to be a distant figure on his tractor and became a demanding producer/ director, inspired Evil Vizier and occasional artistic diva as he drove a mixed bag of talent to practise their scenes. Mr Addington had added the job of health and safety advisor to his role as the front half of Buttercup. He called us together for a 'Safety Briefing', which may have been safe but certainly wasn't brief. He concluded with, "So remember to move around the stage with care, bend your knees when you lift scenery and, of course, no confectionery is to be thrown into the audience!" Ben, who had been dozing, suddenly woke up and looked interested. Mrs Addington was in charge of props, and when Aladdin's plastic lamp broke during the dress rehearsal, she grudgingly produced a valuable antique lamp of her own to replace it. The curtain was ready to rise on our pantomime.

On opening (and indeed closing) night, Ben had planted some friends among the audience to encourage everyone to get in panto mood with their loud, easy laughter, but he needn't have bothered. The village guffawed at the jokes and joined in with gusto when the opportunity arose for audience participation. Annabel skipped prettily around the stage in fishnet tights, but her treatment of Mrs Addington's treasured lamp was casual and the occasional flash of horn-rimmed glasses from the back end of Buttercup showed the situation was being closely monitored. Then, during a comic laundry scene, Widow Twankey (aka Ben) suddenly whipped out an enormous bag of sweets and started tossing them into the crowd. Mr Addington's head popped up from the front of Buttercup, and he shuffled towards the scene of the outrage with moustache bristling ("He's behind you! He's behind you!" chanted the audience). Annabel, delighted by the pink shrimps and fruit salad chews hurtling through the air, abandoned the lamp on the edge of a straw bale and joined in the fun. The lamp teetered and Mrs Addington gave a scream of alarm, then there was a dreadful ripping noise and Buttercup went her two separate ways. Widow Twankey ran around the stage, giggling and hurling sweets as Mr Addington pursued him delivering (at volume) unscripted lines on a health and safety theme, while Mrs Addington – trailing her udder – dived to save her lamp. The audience went wild and it was some time before the Evil Vizier restored order. Anna, the postmistress turned wardrobe mistress, quickly mended Buttercup and the show went on, with the audience munching appreciatively on Ben's largesse.

All in all, it was a night to remember and one day in the future, newcomers to the village will be told of our pantomime, with hoots of laughter. I am so glad that I was there – and I did love it.

Under the Hammer

Mr and Mrs Addington do not have central heating in their house because they fear it would warp their antique furniture, so they are immune to the permafrost that rules in our stone church for much of the year. Decades of fundraising have failed to produce the resources for proper radiators, so Rachael the churchwarden rises early on winter Sunday mornings to fire up the electric heaters. After one particularly icy service, Julia the hedge-fund manager shivered inside several expensive layers of clothing, watched the Addingtons stride briskly away and said that it was high time that the village concentrated on raising some serious money for extra warmth.

Julia is an effective organiser so we transferred to her kitchen table to discuss her proposal that the well-loved but financially inept amusements of the forthcoming village Christmas Party should be replaced by an Auction of Promises, which could convert goods and services into hard cash for church radiators. She started the ball rolling by promising a sumptuous festive hamper, then Colin offered up a week in his Pembrokeshire holiday cottage, while Rachael promised to cook a special meal. Audrey, deadly serious about everything horticultural, then suggested that she could contribute flower arrangements for an Occasion.

Further offers from villagers came rolling in. They ranged from the esoteric (a tour of the vicar's sewage-reed beds, complete with explanatory leaflet) to those strictly for the connoisseur (a day's ferreting with Frank). I considered and discarded riding lessons on Jigsaw, my rampant cob (too dangerous) or a box of garden produce and settled on offering myself and husband to wait at a supper party. Julia insisted that we all kit ourselves out in something relevant to the promise we were offering.

On the big night, I stood nervously behind the curtains on the village hall stage waiting to be auctioned by Colin, our compère for the evening. I was wearing a little black dress and a frilly apron, while my husband was resplendent in his dinner jacket complete with a novelty waterproof apron, to reflect his joint future roles as butler and washer-up. Frank had dressed in floppy bunny ears and powder puff tail, though his ferreting day was more likely to be spent staunching the successful bidder's wounds – Frank's ferrets are quick on the draw – than hassling the local rabbits. Audrey was wearing a hat built of silk flowers, while farmer Maurice (offering 20 bales of meadow hay) was working a rustic look with an ancient ploughman's smock.

I was quietly terrified of being 'bought' by Mr and Mrs Addington for one of their macrobiotic gatherings, but to my huge relief Julia paid handsomely for our services at a future dinner party, complete with Rachael's cooking, and flower arrangements by Audrey. My work over, I joined the audience. Mrs Addington was on stage in evening dress to reflect the generous offer of her close-harmony singing group performing in the comfort of somebody's sitting room. "You'll need ear plugs with that lot yelling at you close up," muttered Frank. He was equally unimpressed by Mr Addington's offer to research

the history of any specified village house ("Nosy old git!"). Next up was Julia's luxury hamper from a famous London store. Colin handed over the role of auctioneer to Rachael and joined the bidding, securing the gourmet goods after a close-fought battle with Maurice.

The auction was nearing its close, and last on was the vicar. He shuffled onto the stage wearing a hopeful smile and a hat woven by his wife from sewage-bed reeds. Bidding hung unaccountably slack and I heard myself offer £20 for his guided tour. All too soon the lot was knocked down to me. It's in a good cause: radiators for the church are now an achievable reality rather than an impossible dream. And as for the future promise of a happy afternoon spent studying the vicar's little hobby – well, I can hardly wait!

Season's Meetings

Our village Christmas party started as it always did: with Ralph, the oldest inhabitant, backing his small red car with shaky determination right across the car park of the Friendly Ferret and into the stone mounting block that stands next to the pub's front door. Unsurprisingly, the block held firm and Ralph's car, sporting an impressive dent, shot forwards and began to ricochet around the car park. It finally came to rest among the wheelie bins, and only then was it safe for the rest of us to approach the pub and go inside.

We gathered in the bar, which was richly decorated with tinsel, to order drinks and enter bids for the Silent Auction. As well as such sure-fire successes as the Christmas tree from Colin's little plantation, a basket of produce from the farm shop and a load of firewood donated by Frank, there was the kind offer of six half-hour maths lessons with Mrs Addington. Now, Mrs Addington has many virtues, but the prospect of being closeted with her for three hours would have everybody in the village running for cover.

As the evening continued, and the bidding forms filled up (proceeds towards the fund for heating the church above freezing point), the Addington maths paper remained stubbornly blank. Some of us had a whispered crisis meeting behind a gigantic paper lantern. It would be unthinkable for the offer to be returned, but who should be the sacrificial victim? Maurice finally solved the problem. His daughter Emily would probably agree to the lessons if she were offered a trip to Longleat Safari Park with unfettered access to the gift shop as a sweetener.

Next up was the 'What happened next?' competition, a popular feature of our Christmas party. Snapshots taken during the year were on display, and villagers had to remember, or guess, how the action continued after the photograph was taken. The first photo showed Ralph hobbling happily down the street clutching a croquet mallet. (I knew this one – he was off to do some panel beating on his little car.) The second showed Colin wearing a gleaming white bee-keeper's outfit. Ben, standing next to me, giggled and related what happened next. Colin's latest attempt at beekeeping had backfired when the new bees had decided against their luxury hive, voted with their wings and swarmed. Colin had looked up what to do in his bee book, did it wrong and panicked. The bees had been gaining the upper hand when Frank had spotted the commotion and, wearing nothing more protective than old cords and an open-necked shirt, had taken the swarm off to one of his battered old hives. The bees had immediately settled in and were now producing industrial quantities of honey. It was still possible (said Ben) to make Colin flinch by buzzing at him.

We continued to the third photo, which showed me running along the road with a bucket of sheep feed with my flock streaming behind me. This is how I move my sheep between fields and it usually works a treat. But just after Anna took the photograph, Maurice came around the corner on his tractor and the sheep scattered in every direction. Some ended up in the village, where they ate all the roses in Audrey's garden which was shortly to be opened to the public. The others reached the only significant road in the vicinity where they disrupted traffic until I arrived panting with my bucket. It had been an emotional day, and I continued with relief onto the next photograph where Maurice (the eventual winner of the free-range turkey) was dressed as a fairy princess. No idea what that was about, but I have noticed that the bigger and hairier the farmer, the quicker they are to put on a tutu.

After the carol singing, Ben decided to say a few words. He'd been helping himself lavishly to Christmas cheer, so we regarded him apprehensively as he cleared his throat. "You're a funny old lot," he said thoughtfully, his glance lingering on the disapproving face of Mr Addington, "but you're my mates and this is a great village. Happy Christmas!" And, thinking about it, I couldn't have put it better myself.

Ben's Christmas Cheer

Christmas comes but once a year and I like to make the most of it. I'm behind the village hall bar at our annual Christmas bash and (though I say it myself) when it comes to getting a party going with a swing in a very short time, I'm your man! Guests arrive feeling chilly, I press a glass of something warming into their hands and the deed is done. You'd be scraping them off the floor at 4am next morning if they had their way. The trick is to get that first glass right. Give them something that would pep up an elephant before they've got time to say no really they've got to get back to write Christmas cards. Get a glass of Ben's Christmas Blaster down their necks pronto and they'll be hanging off the chandeliers at chucking-out time. Trust me on this one. They're all walking home, or crawling more like, so there's no problem there. And of course there's always a non-alcoholic alternative. Ho ho ho!

Ben's Christmas Blaster

For every litre bottle of fruity red wine add:

100ml port
Slug of brandy
1 orange cut in half, each half studded with about 4 cloves
1 stick cinnamon
Pinch nutmeg
1 tbsp honey

Heat until very hot but not boiling and (this is important) taste it. You might want to add more spices, or a glass of ginger wine, or a cup of black tea. Suck it and see, and then you'll be nice and festive for your guests when they arrive. It's win-win, really. As far as quantities go, I allow half a bottle of wine per person, which seems to do the trick.

Merry Christmas one and all!

Addington's Alternative (non-alcoholic)

For the Addingtons, anybody who's driving and anybody who doesn't appreciate my Blaster.

For every litre carton of red grape juice add:

500ml orange juice
1 orange cut in half, each half studded with about 4 cloves
1 stick cinnamon
Pinch nutmeg
1 tbsp honey
Some slices of root ginger, peeled

Heat until very hot but not boiling and serve.

When Mr Addington's had a couple of these I distract his attention and slip him glass of the Blaster. Only joking. Actuall I give him two glasses. That'll carry him through Christmas Day with Her.